Anonymous

**The Adventurer**

Vol. III

Anonymous

**The Adventurer**
*Vol. III*

ISBN/EAN: 9783337176907

Printed in Europe, USA, Canada, Australia, Japan

Cover: Foto ©ninafisch / pixelio.de

More available books at **www.hansebooks.com**

# THE

# ADVENTURER.

## VOLUME THE THIRD.

*——Tentanda via est; quá me quoque possim*
*Tollere humo, victorque virúm volitare per ora.*
                                        VIRG.

On vent'rous wing in quest of praise I go,
And leave the gazing multitude below.

## A NEW EDITION.

### ILLUSTRATED WITH FRONTISPIECES.

## LONDON:

Printed for W. STRAHAN, J. RIVINGTON and Sons,
J. DODSLEY, T. LONGMAN, B. LAW, T. CASLON,
T. LOWNDES, J. WILKIE, T. CADELL, T. DAVIES,
T. BECKET, W. FLEXNEY, F. NEWBERY, W. GOLD-
SMITH, W. NICOLL, W. STEWART, N. CONANT,
W. FOX, and E. JOHNSTON.

M.DCC.LXXVIII.

# CONTENTS

## OF THE

## THIRD VOLUME.

# CONTENTS OF THE THIRD VOLUME.

THE

# THE

# ADVENTURER.

Numb. 71.   Tuesday, *July* 10, 1753.

——*Hominem pagina nostra sapit.*   Mart.

We strive to paint the manners and the mind.

LETTERS written from the heart and on real occasions, though not always decorated with the flowers of eloquence, must be far more useful and interesting than the studied paragraphs of Pliny, or the pompous declamations of Balsac; as they contain just pictures of life and manners, and are the genuine emanations of nature. Of this kind I shall select a few from the heap I have received from my correspondents, each of which exhibits a different character, not exaggerated and heightened by circumstances that pass the bounds of reality.

Vol. III.            B                    To

To the ADVENTURER.

SIR,        Sombre-Hall, June 18.

I AM arrived with Sir Nicholas at this melancholy moated manfion. Would I could be annihilated during the infupportable tedioufnefs of fummer! We are to fup this evening, after having fifhed the whole afternoon, by day-light, think of that, in the new arbour. My uncle, poor man, imagines he has a finer and richer profpect from thence, than the illuminated viftas at Vauxhall afford, only becaufe he fees a parcel of woods and meadows, and blue hills, and cornfields. We have been vifited by our only neighbour, Mrs. Thrifty, who entertained us with a dull hiftory of the children fhe has educated at a little fchool of her own founding, and who values herfelf for not having been in town thefe ten years, and for not knowing what a drum means. My fifter and I have laid a fcheme to plague her, for we have fent her a card, entreating her to make one at Brag next Sunday. For heaven's fake fend us your paper weekly, but do not give us fo many grave ones; for we want to be diverted after ftudying Hoyle, which we do for three hours every afternoon with great attention, that the time may not pafs away totally ufelefs, and that we may be a match for Lady SHUFFLE

next

next winter.   Let us know what is done at the
next Jubilee Mafquerade.   How fhall I have
patience to fupport my abfence from it! And if
Madam de Pompadour comes over, as was reported when I left town, impart to us a minute
account of the complexion fhe now wears, and
of every article of her drefs : any milliner will
explain the terms to you.   I don't fee that you
have yet publifhed the little novel I fent you ; I
affure you it was written by a right honourable :
but you, I fuppofe, think the ftyle colloquial as
you call it, and the moral trite or trifling.   Co-
lonel Caper's pindaric ode on the E O table,
muft abfolutely be inferted in your very next
paper, or elfe never expect to hear again from

LETITIA.

To the ADVENTURER.

SIR,

I Apply to you, as a perfon of prudence and
knowledge of the world, for directions how
to extricate myfelf out of a great and uncommon
difficulty.   To enable myfelf to breed up a numerous family on a fmall preferment, I have been ad-
vifed to indulge my natural propenfity for poetry,
and to write a tragedy : my defign is to apprentice
my eldeft fon to a reputable tradefman, with the
profits I fhall acquire by the reprefentation of my

B 2                              play,

play, being deterred by the inordinate expences
of an Univerſity education from making him a
ſcholar. An old gentlewoman in my pariſh, a
great reader of religious controverſy, whom celi-
bacy and the reduction of intereſt have made
moroſely devout, accidentally hearing of my performance, undertook to cenſure me in all com-
panies with acrimony and zeal, as acting incon-
ſiſtently with the dignity of my public character,
and as a promoter of debauchery and lewdneſs.
She has informed my church-wardens, that the
playhouſe is the temple of Satan, and that the
firſt Chriſtians were ſtrictly forbidden to enter the
theatres, as places impure and contagious. My
congregations grow thin ; my clerk ſhakes his
head, and fears his maſter is not ſo ſound as he
ought to be. I was lately diſcourſing on the
beautiful parable of the prodigal ſon, and moſt
unfortunately quoted ERASMUS's obſervation on
it, " ex quo quidem argumento poſſet non inele-
" gans texi comedia,—on which ſubject a moſt
" elegant comedy might be compoſed ;" which
has ruined me for ever, and deſtroyed all the little
reſpect remaining for me in the minds of my
pariſhioners. What! cried they, would the
parſon put the Bible into verſe ? would he make
ſtage-plays out of the Scriptures ? How, Sir, am
I to act ? Aſſiſt me with your advice. Am I for
ever to bear unreaſonable obloquy, and unde-
ſerved

ferved reproach? or muft I, to regain the good
opinion of my people, relinquifh all hopes of
the five hundred pounds I was to gain by my
piece, and generoufly burn my tragedy in my
church-yard, in the face of my whole congre-
gation?

Yours, &c.

JACOB THOMASON.

To the ADVENTURER.

SIR,

I Had almoft finifhed a view of the infide of
St. Peter's at Rome in BUTTERFLY-WORK,
when my cruel parroquet accidentally trod upon
the PURPLE EMPEROR, of which the high altar
was to have been made.   This is the firft letter
I have written after my dreadful lofs; and it is
to defire you to put an advertifement at the end
of your next paper, fignifying, that whoever has
any " purple emperors or fwallow tails" to difpofe of, may hear of a purchafer at Lady WHIM's
in New Bond ftreet.

Your's, &c.

B 3

## To the ADVENTURER.

SIR,

I F you will pay off my milk-fcore and lodgings, ftop my taylor from arrefting me, and
put twenty pieces in my pocket, I will immediately fet out for Lyons on foot, and ftay there
till I have tranflated into Englifh the manufcript
of LONGINUS which you talk of in your fifty-
firft paper. Favour me with a fpeedy anfwer,
directed to Mr. QUILLIT, at the cork-cutter's
in Wych-ftreet, Drury-lane.

P. S. Seven bookfellers have already applied
to me, and offer to pay me very generoufly for
my tranflation, efpecially as there is no French
one for me to confult.

## To the ADVENTURER.

SIR,

Y OU affect great tendernefs and fenfibility
whenever you fpeak of the ladies. I have
always defpifed them as trifling and expenfive
animals; and have, therefore, enjoyed the delicious liberty of what they idly and opprobrioufly
call an old bachelor. I confider love in no other
light, than as the parent of mifery and folly, and
the fon of idlenefs and eafe. I am, therefore,
inexpreffibly delighted with a paffage of uncommon

mon fenfe and penetration, which I lately met with in the works of the celebrated Huet; and which, becaufe no Englifh writer has taken notice of it, I beg you would publifh for the ufe of my countrymen, as it will impart to them a method of efcaping the defpicable lot of living under female tyranny.

"Love," fays this judicious prelate, "is not
"only a paffion of the foul like hatred and
"envy, but is alfo a malady of the body like a
"fever. It is fituated in the blood and the
"animal fpirits, which are extraordinarily in-
"flamed and agitated; and it ought to be treated
"methodically by the rules of medicine, in or-
"der to effect a cure. I am of opinion, that
"this diforder may eafily be fubdued by plenti-
"ful fweats and copious bleedings, which
"would carry off the peccant humours and
"thefe violent inflammations, would purge the
"blood, calm its emotion, and re-eftablifh it
"in its former natural ftate. This is not merely
"groundlefs conjecture, it is an opinion founded
"on experience. A great prince, with whom
"I was intimately acquainted, having conceived
"a violent paffion for a young lady of exalted
"merit, was obliged to leave her, and to take
"the field with the army. During this abfence,
"his love was cherifhed and kept alive by a very
"frequent and regular intercourfe of letters to

" the end of the campaign, when a dangerous
" ficknefs reduced him to extremity.   By ap-
" plying to the moft powerful and efficacious
" drugs phyfic could boaft of, he recovered his
" health, but loft his paffion, which the great
" evacuations he had ufed had entirely carried
" off unknown to him.   For imagining that he
" was as much in love as ever, he found himfelf
" unexpectedly cold and indifferent, the firft
" time he beheld again the lady of whom he
" had been fo paffionately fond.   The like ac-
" cident befel one of my moft intimate friends,
" who recovering from a long and ftubborn
" fever by falling into copious fweats, per-
" ceived at the fame time that he was cured of
" a paffion, that for fome time before had con-
" tinually teized and grievoufly tormented him.
" He had no longer any tafte for the object he
" formerly adored, attempted in vain to re-
" new his gallantries, and found that infenfi-
" bility and diflike had banifhed tendernefs and
" refpect."

I am yours, .

A K A L O S.

## To the ADVENTURER.

SIR,

IN one of your late sermons I am informed, for I never read myself, that you have presumed to speak with ridicule and contempt of the noble order of BUCKS. Seven of us agreed last night at the King's Arms, that if you dared to be guilty of the like impudence a second time, we would come in a body and untile your garret, burn your pocket-book of hints, throw your papers ready written for the press into a jakes, and drive you out into the Strand in your tattered night-gown and slippers: and you may guess what a fine spectacle the mob will think an animal that so seldom sees the sun as you do. I assure you, that next to a day at Broughton's, or the damnation of a new play, the truest joy of our fraternity is, " to hunt an author."

Yours,

Z

BOB WHIPCLEAN,

NUMB. 72.  SATURDAY, *July* 14, 1753.

Πόλλα μῖαξὺ πίλιι κάλυκος καὶ χιίλιος ἀκρῶ.

PROV. GR.

Many things happen between the cup and the lip.

THE following narrative is by an eastern tradition attributed to one HELI BEN HAMET, a moralist of Arabia, who is said to have delivered his precepts in public and periodical orations. This tradition corresponds with the manner in which the narrative is introduced; and, indeed, it may possibly have no other foundation: but the tradition itself, however founded, is sufficient authority to consider HELI as the literary ADVENTURER of a remote age and nation; and as only one number of his work is extant, I shall not scruple to incorporate it with my own.

DOST thou ask a torch to discover the brightness of the morning? dost thou appeal to argument for proofs of DIVINE PERFECTION? Look down to the earth on which thou standest, and lift up thine eye to the worlds that roll above thee. Thou beholdest splendor, abundance, and beauty; is not HE who produced them MIGHTY? Thou considerest; is not HE who formed thy under-

understanding, WISE ? Thou enjoyeſt; is not
HE who gratifies thy ſenſes, GOOD ? Can aught
have limited his bounty but his wiſdom ? or can
defects in his ſagacity be diſcovered by thine ?
To HELI, the preacher of humility and reſig-
nation, let thine ear be again attentive, thou
whoſe heart has rebelled in ſecret, and whoſe
wiſh has ſilently accuſed thy MAKER.

I ROSE early in the morning to meditate,
that I might without preſumption hope to be
heard. I left my habitation, and, turning from
the beaten path, I wandered without remarking
my way, or regarding any object that I paſſed,
till the extreme heat of the ſun, which now approached the meridian, compelled my attention.
The wearineſs which I had inſenſibly contracted
by the length of my walk, became in a moment
inſupportable; and looking round for ſhelter, I
ſuddenly perceived that I was not far from the
wood, in which RHEDI the hermit inveſtigates
the ſecrets of nature, and aſcribes glory to GOD.
The hope of improving my meditation by his
wiſdom, gave me new vigour; I ſoon reached
the wood, I was refreſhed by the ſhade, and I
walked forward till I reached the cell. I entered,
but RHEDI was abſent. I had not, however,
waited long, before I diſcovered him through
the trees at ſome diſtance, advancing towards me
with a perſon whoſe appearance was, if poſ-

ſible,

fible, yet more venerable, and whom before I had never feen.

WHEN they came near I rofe up, and laying my hand upon my lips, I bowed myfelf with reverence before them. RHEDI faluted me by my name, and prefented me to his companion, before whom I again bowed myfelf to the ground. Having looked ftedfaftly in my countenance, he laid his hand upon my head, and bleffed me: "HELI," faid he, "thofe who defire KNOW- "LEDGE that they may teach VIRTUE, fhall "not be difappointed: fit down, I will relate "events which yet thou knoweft but in part, "and difclofe fecrets of PROVIDENCE from "which thou mayeft derive inftruction." We fat down, and I liftened as to the counfel of an Angel, or the mufic of Paradife.

AMANA, the daughter of SANBAD the fhep- berd, was drawing water at the wells of Adail, when a caravan which had paffed the defart ar- rived, and the driver of the camels alighted to give them drink: thofe which came firft to the wells, belonged to NOURADDIN the merchant, who had brought fine linen and other merchan- dize of great value from Egypt. AMANA, when the caravan drew near, had covered herfelf with her veil, which the fervant of NOURADDIN, to gratify a brutal curiofity, attempted to with- draw.

†

AMANA,

AMANA, provoked by the indignity, and encouraged by the presence of others, struck him with the staff of the bucket; and he was about to retaliate the violence, when NOURADDIN, who was himself with the caravan, called out to him to forbear, and immediately hasted to the well. The veil of AMANA had fallen off in the struggle, and NOURADDIN was captivated with her beauty: the lovely confusion of offended modesty that glowed upon her cheek, the disdain that swelled her bosom, and the resentment that sparkled in her eyes, expressed a consciousness of her sex, which warmed and animated her beauty: they were graces which NOURADDIN had never seen, and produced a tumult in his breast which he had never felt; for NOURADDIN, though he had now great possessions, was yet a youth, and a stranger to woman: the merchandize which he was transporting, had been purchased by his father, whom the angel of death had intercepted in the journey, and the sudden accession of independence and wealth did not dispose him to restrain the impetuosity of desire: he, therefore, demanded AMANA of her parents; his message was received with gratitude and joy; and NOURADDIN, after a short time, carried her back to Egypt, having first punished the servant, by whom she had been insulted at the well, with his own hand.

BUT

BUT he delayed the folemnities of marriage, till the time of mourning for his father fhould expire; and the gratification of a paffion which he could not fupprefs, was without much difficulty fufpended now its object was in his power. He anticipated the happinefs which he believed to be fecured; and fuppofed that it would increafe by expectation, like a treafure by ufury, of which more is ftill poffeffed, as poffeffion is longer delayed.

DURING this interval AMANA recovered from the tumultuous joy of fudden elevation; her ambition was at an end, and fhe became fufceptible of love. NOURADDIN, who regretted the obfcurity of her birth only becaufe it had prevented the cultivation of her mind, laboured inceffantly to fupply the defect: fhe received his inftruction not only with gratitude, but delight; while he fpoke fhe gazed upon him with efteem and reverence, and had no wifh but to return the happinefs which he was impatient to beftow.

AT this time OSMIN the Caliph was upon the throne of Egypt. The paffions of OSMIN, thou knoweft, were impetuous as the torrents of Alared, and fatal as the whirlwind of the defart: to excite and to gratify, was the whole purpofe of his mind; but his wifh was ftill unfatisfied, and his life was wretched. His feraglio was filled with beauty; but the power of beauty he had exhaufted:

exhaufted : he became outrageous to revive dé-
fire by a new object, which he demanded of
Nardic the eunuch, whom he had. not only fet
over his women but his kingdom, with menaces
and execration.  ·Nardic, therefore, caufed a
proclamation to be made, that whoever fhould
produce the moft beautiful virgin within two
days, fhould ftand in the prefence of the CALIPH,
and be deemed the third in his kingdom.

CALED, the fervant who had been beaten by
NOURADDIN, returned with him to Egypt : the
fullen ferocity of his temper was increafed by the
defire of revenge, and the gloom of difcontent
was deepened by defpair : but when he heard the
proclamation of Nardic, joy kindled in his afpect
like lightning in the darknefs of a ftorm ; the
offence which he had committed againft AMANA,
enabled him to revenge the punifhment which it
produced.   He knew that fhe was yet a virgin,
and that her marriage was near : he, therefore,
hafted to the palace, and demanded to be brought
before Nardic, who in the midft of magnificence
and fervility, the flattery of dependent ambition
and the zeal of unlimited obedience, was fitting
pale and filent, his brow contracted with anxiety,
and his breaft throbbing with apprehenfion.

WHEN Caled was brought into his prefence,
he fell proftrate before him : " By the fmile of
" my Lord," faid he, " let another be diftin-
" guifhed

" guished from the slaves who mingle in obscu-
" rity, and let his favour elevate another from the
" dust; but let my service be accepted, and let
" the desire of OSMIN be satisfied with beauty.
" AMANA will shortly be espoused by NOURAD-
" DIN; but of AMANA the sovereign of Egypt
" only is worthy. Haste, therefore, to demand
" her; she is now with him in the house, to which
" I will conduct the messenger of thy will."

NARDIC received this intelligence with trans-
ports of joy; a mandate was instantly written to
NOURADDIN; it was sealed with the royal signet,
and delivered to Caled, who returned with a
force sufficient to compel obedience.

ON this day the mourning of NOURADDIN
expired : he had changed his apparel, and per-
fumed his person; his features were brightened
with the gladness of his heart; he had invited
his friends to the festival of his marriage, and
the evening was to accomplish his wishes : the
evening also was expected by AMANA, with a
joy which she did not labour to suppress; and
she was hiding her blushes in the breast of NOU-
RADDIN, when Caled arrived with the mandate
and the guard.

THE domestics were alarmed and terrified;
and NOURADDIN, being instantly acquainted
with the event, rushed out of the apartment of
AMANA with disorder and trepidation. When
he

he faw Caled, he was moved with anger and difdain; but he was intimidated by the appearance
of the guard. Caled immediately advanced,
and, with looks of infolence and triumph, prefented the mandate. NOURADDIN feeing the
royal fignet, kneeled to receive it; and having
gazed a moment at the fuperfcription, preffed it
upon his forehead in an agony of fufpence and
terror. The wretch who had betrayed him enjoyed the anguifh which he fuffered; and perceiving that he was fainting, and had not fortitude to read the paper, acquainted him with the
contents: at the name of AMANA he ftarted, as
if he had felt the fting of a fcorpion, and immediately fell to the ground.

CALED proceeded to execute his commiffion
without remorfe; he was not to be moved by
fwooning, expoftulation, entreaty, or tears; but
having conducted AMANA to the feraglio, prefented her to Nardic, with exultation and hope.
Nardic, whofe wifh was flattered by her ftature
and her fhape, lifted up her veil with impatience,
timidity, and folicitude: but the moment he
beheld her face, his doubts were at an end: he
proftrated himfelf before her, as a perfon on
whofe pleafure his life would from that moment
depend. She was conducted to the chamber of
the women, and Caled was the fame hour invefted with his new dignity; an apartment was
affigned

affigned him in the palace, and he was made captain of the guard that kept the gates.

NOURADDIN, when he recovered his fenfibility, and found that AMANA had been conducted to the feraglio, was feized by turns with diftraction and ftupidity : he paffed the night in agitations, by which the powers of nature were exhaufted, and in the morning he locked himfelf into the chamber of AMANA, and threw himfelf on a fofa, determined to admit no comforter, and to receive no fuftenance.

\* \* \* \* \* \* \* \* \* \* \* \* \* \* \* \* \* \* \* \* \* \* \* \* \*

NUMB. 73.   TUESDAY, *July* 17, 1753.

——*Numinibus vota exaudita malignis.*   JUV.
Prayers made and granted in a lucklefs hour.
                                        DRYDEN.

WHILE NOURADDIN was thus abandoned to defpair, Nardic's defcription of AMANA had rouzed OSMIN from his apathy. He commanded that fhe fhould be prepared to receive him, and foon after went alone into her apartment. Familiar as he was with beauty, and fatiated with enjoyment, he could not behold AMANA without emotion : he perceived, indeed, that fhe was in tears, and that his prefence covered her with confufion ; yet he believed that her terrors would be eafily removed, that by
                                        kindnefs

kindnefs fhe might be foothed to familiarity, and by careffes excited to dalliance ; but the moment he approached her, fhe threw herfelf at his feet, and entreated to be heard, with an importunity which he chofe rather to indulge than refift ; he, therefore, raifed her from the ground, and fupporting her in his arms, encouraged her to proceed, " Let my Lord," faid fhe, " difmifs a " wretch who is not worthy of his prefence, " and compaffionate the diftrefs which is not " fufceptible of delight. I am the daughter of a " fhepherd, betrothed to the merchant Nou- " RADDIN, from whom my body has been forced " by the perfidy of a flave, and to whom my " foul is united by indiffoluble bonds. O ! let " not the terrors of thy frown be upon me ! " Shall the fovereign of Egypt ftoop to a rep- " tile of the duft ? fhall the judge of nations " retain the worthlefs theft of treachery and " revenge ? or fhall he, for whom ten thoufand " languifh with defire, rejoice in the fufferance " of one alienated mind ?" OSMIN, whofe breaft had by turns been inflamed with defire and indignation, while he gazed upon the beauties of AMANA and liftened to her voice, now fuddenly threw her from him, and departed without reply.

WHEN he was alone, he remained a few moments in fufpence : but the paffions which eloquence had repreffed, foon became again predominant;

dominant; and he commanded AMANA to be told, that if within three hours she did not come prepared to gratify his wishes, he would cast the head of the slave for whom he was rejected at her feet.

THE eunuch by whom this message was delivered, and the woman who had returned to AMANA when the CALIPH retired, were touched with pity at her distress, and trembled at her danger: the evils which they could scarce hope to prevent, they were yet solicitous to delay; and, therefore, advised her to request three days of preparation, that she might sufficiently recover the tranquillity of her mind, to make a just estimate of her own happiness; and with this request to send, as a pledge of her obedience, a bowl of sherbet, in which a pearl had been dissolved, and of which she had first drank herself.

To this advice, after some throbs of desperation, she at length consented, and prepared to put it in execution.

AT the time when this resolution was taken, NOURADDIN suddenly started from a restless slumber; he was again stung by an instantaneous reflection upon his own misery, and indulged the discontent of his mind in this exclamation: " If " wisdom and goodness do indeed preside over the " works of OMNIPOTENCE, whence is oppres- " sion, injustice, and cruelty? As NOURADDIN " alone

" alone has a right to AMANA, why is AMANA
" in the power of OSMIN ? O that now the juf-
" tice of HEAVEN would appear in my behalf !
" O that from this hour I was OSMIN, and Os-
" MIN NOURADDIN !" The moment he had
uttered this wifh, his chamber was darkened as
with a thick cloud, which was at length diffipated by a búrft of thunder; and a being, whofe
appearance was more than human, ftood before
him. " NOURADDIN," faid the vifion, " I am
" of the region above thee : but my bufinefs is
" with the children of the earth. Thou haft
" wifhed to be OSMIN, and as far as this wifh
" is poffible it fhall be accomplifhed ; thou fhalt
" be enabled to affume his appearance, and to
" exercife his power. I know not yet whether
" I am permitted to conceal OSMIN under the
" appearance of NOURADDIN, but till to-mor-
" row he fhall not interrupt thee."

NOURADDIN, who had been held motionlefs
by aftonifhment and terror, now recovered his
fortitude as in the prefence of a friend ; and was
about to exprefs his gratitude and joy, when the
GENIUS bound a talifman on his left arm, and
acquainted him with its power : " As often as
" this bracelet," faid he, " fhall be applied to
" the region of thy heart, thou fhalt be alter-
" nately changed in appearance from NOURAD-
" DIN to OSMIN, and from OSMIN to NOU-
" RADDIN."

" RADDIN." The Genius then fuddenly difap-
peared, and NOURADDIN, impatient to recover
the poffeffion of AMANA, inftantly applied the
ftud of the bracelet to his breaft, and the next
moment found himfelf alone in an apartment of
the feraglio.

DURING this interval, the CALIPH, who was
expecting the iffue of his meffage to AMANA,
became reftlefs and impatient : he quitted his
apartment, and went into the gardens, where
he walked backward and forward with a violent
but interrupted pace ; and at length ftood ftill,
frowning and penfive, with his eyes fixed on the
clear furface of a fountain in the middle of the
walk. The agitation of his mind continued,
and at length broke out into this foliloquy :
" What is my felicity, and what is my power ?
" I am wretched, by the want of that which
" the caprice of women has beftowed upon my
" flave. I can gratify revenge, but not defire ;
" I can with-hold felicity from him, but I cannot
" procure it to myfelf. Why have I not power
" to affume the form in which I might enjoy my
" wifhes ? I will at leaft enjoy them in thought.
" If I was NOURADDIN, I fhould be clafped
" with tranfport to the bofom of AMANA."
He then refigned himfelf to the power of imagination, and was again filent : but the moment
his wifh was uttered, he became fubject to the

GENIUS

GENIUS who had juſt tranſported NOURADDIN
to his palace. This wiſh, therefore, was inſtantly fulfilled; and his eyes being ſtill fixed
upon the water, he perceived, with ſudden wonder and delight, that his figure had been changed
in a moment, and that the mirror reflected another image. His fancy had been warmed with
the ideal careſſes of AMANA; the tumult of his
mind was increaſed by the prodigy; and the
gratification of his appetite being the only object of his attention, he haſted inſtantly to the
palace, without reflecting that, as he would not
be known, he would be refuſed admittance.
At the door, to which he advanced with eager-
neſs and precipitation, he was ſtopped by a party
of the guard that was now commanded by
Caled: a tumult enſued, and Caled being
haſtily called, believed that NOURADDIN, in
the phrenzy of deſperation, had ſcaled the walls
of the garden to recover AMANA; and rejoicing
in an opportunity of revenge that exceeded his
hope, inſtantly ſtabbed him with his poinard,
but at the ſame time received that of the CA-
LIPH in his heart. Thus fell at once the tyrant
and the traitor; the tyrant by the hand which
had been armed to ſupport him in oppreſſion,
and the traitor by the fury of the appetite which
his perfidy had excited.

In

In the mean time the man who was believed to be flain, repofed in fecurity upon a fofa; and AMANA, by the direction of her women, had prepared the meffage and the bowl. They were now difpatched to the CALIPH, and received by NOURADDIN. He underftood by the meffage that AMANA was yet inviolate: in the joy of his heart, therefore, he took the bowl, which having emptied, he returned by the eunuch, and commanded that AMANA fhould be brought into his prefence.

In obedience to this command, fhe was con-ducted by her women to the door, but fhe en-tered alone pale and trembling; and though her lips were forced into a fmile, the characters which grief, dread and averfion, had written in her countenance, were not effaced. NOURADDIN, who beheld her diforder, exulted in the fidelity of her love, and fpringing forward, threw his arms about her in an extafy of tendernefs and joy; which was ftill heightened when he per-ceived, that in the character of OSMIN thofe embraces were fuffered with reluctance, which in his own were returned with ardor: he, there-fore, retreating backward a few paces, applied the talifman again to his breaft, and having re-covered his own form, would have rufhed again into her arms; but fhe ftarted from him in con-fufion and terror. He fmiled at the effect of the

prodigy;

prodigy; and suftaining her on his bofom, repeated fome tender incidents which were known to no other; told her by what means he had intercepted her meffage; and urged her immediately to efcape, that they might poffefs all their defires in each other, and leave the incumbrance of royalty to the wretch whofe likenefs he had been enabled to affume, and was now impatient to renounce. AMANA gazed at him with a fixed attention, till her fufpicion and doubts were removed; then fuddenly turned from him, tore her garment, and looking up to heaven, imprecated curfes upon her head, till her voice faultered, and fhe burft into tears.

OF this agony, which NOURADDIN beheld with unutterable diftrefs, the broken exclamations of AMANA at length acquainted him with the caufe. " In the bowl," faid fhe, " which " thou haft intercepted, there was death. I " wifhed, when I took it from my lips, that the " draught which remained might be poifon: " a powder was immediately fhaken into it by " an invifible hand, and a voice whifpered me, " that him who drank the potion it would in- " evitably deftroy."

NOURADDIN, to whofe heart the fatal malignity had now fpread, perceived that his diffolution would be fudden: his legs already trembled, and his eyes became dim: he ftretched

out his arms towards AMANA, and his countenance was diftorted by an ineffectual effort to
fpeak; impenetrable darknefs came upon him,
he groaned and fell backwards. In his fall the
talifman again fmote his breaft; his form was
again changed, and the horrors of death were
impreffed upon the features of OSMIN. AMANA,
who ran to fupport him, when fhe perceived
the laft transformation, rufhed out of the apartment with the wild impetuofity of diftraction
and defpair. The feraglio was alarmed in a
moment: the body, which was miftaken for that
of OSMIN, was examined by the phyficians;
the effects of poifon were evident; AMANA
was immediately fufpected; and by the command of SHOMAR, who fucceeded his father,
fhe was put to death.

"Such," faid the companion of RHEDI,
"was the end of NOURADDIN and AMANA,
"of OSMIN and CALED, from whofe deftiny
"I have withdrawn the veil: let the world
"confider it, and be wife. Be thou ftill the
"meffenger of inftruction, and let increafe of
"knowledge cloath thee with humility."

WHILE mine eye was fixed upon the hoary
fage, who had thus vouchfafed me counfel and
knowledge, his countenance became bright as
the morning, and his robe fleecy like a cloud;

†                  he

he rofe like a vapour from the ground, and the next moment I faw him no more.

I THEN turned towards RHEDI the hermit, chilled with reverence, and dumb with aftonifhment: but in the countenance of RHEDI was the calm chearfulnefs of fuperior virtue; and I perceived that the fanctity of his life had acquainted him with divine intelligence. "HA-
"MET," faid he, "the voice which thou haft
"heard, is the voice of ZACHIS the genius;
"by whofe power the wonders which he has
"related were produced. It is the province of
"ZACHIS to punifh impatience and prefump-
"tion, by fulfilling the defires of thofe who
"wifh to interrupt the order of nature, and
"prefume to direct the hand of PROVIDENCE.
"Relate what thou haft heard, to preferve
"others from his power."

Now, therefore, let VIRTUE fuffer adverfity with patience, and VICE dread to incur the mifery fhe would inflict: for by him who repines at the fcale of HEAVEN, his own portion of good is diminifhed; and he who prefumptuoufly affumes the fword, will turn the point upon his own bofom.

NUMB. 74.    SATURDAY, *July* 21, 1753.

*Infanientis dum fapientiæ*
*Confultus, erro.*                         HOR.

I miſt my end, and loſt my way,
By crack-brain'd wiſdom led aſtray.

To the ADVENTURER.

SIR,

IT has long been charged by one part of mankind upon the other, that they will not take
advice; that counſel and inſtruction are generally
thrown away; and that, in defiance both of
admonition and example, all claim the right to
chuſe their own meaſures, and to regulate their
own lives.

THAT there is ſomething in advice very uſeful and ſalutary, ſeems to be equally confeſſed on
all hands; ſince even thoſe that reject it, allow
for the moſt part that rejection to be wrong, but
charge the fault upon the unſkilful manner in
which it is given; they admit the efficacy of the
medicine, but abhor the nauſeouſneſs of the
vehicle.

THUS mankind have gone on from century to
century: ſome have been adviſing others how
to act, and ſome have been teaching the adviſers
how to adviſe; yet very little alteration has been
                                        made

made in the world.   As we muſt all by the law
of nature enter life in ignorance, we muſt all
make our way through it by the light of our own
experience ; and, for any ſecurity that advice
has been yet able to afford, muſt endeavour after
ſucceſs at the hazard of miſcarriage, and learn
to do right. by venturing to do wrong.

BY advice I would not be underſtood to mean,
the everlaſting and invariable principles of moral
and religious truth, from which no change of
external circumſtances can juſtify any deviation ;
but ſuch directions as reſpect merely the pru-
dential part of conduct, and which may be followed or neglected without any violation of
eſſential duties.

IT is, indeed, not ſo frequently to make us
good as to make us wiſe, that our friends employ the officiouſneſs of counſel ; and among the
rejectors of advice, who are mentioned by the
grave and ſententious with ſo much acrimony,
you will not ſo often find the vicious and abandoned, as the pert and the petulant, the viva-
cious and the giddy.

As the great end of female education is to get
a huſband, this likewiſe is the general ſubject of
female advice ; and the dreadful denunciation
againſt thoſe volatile girls, who will not liſten
patiently to the lectures of wrinkled wiſdom, is,
that they will die unmarried, or throw themſelves

C 3                        away

away upon fome worthlefs fellow, who will never be able to keep them a coach.

I BEING naturally of a ductile and eafy temper, without ftrong defires or quick refentments, was always a favourite amongft the elderly ladies, becaufe I never rebelled againft feniority, nor could be charged with thinking myfelf wife before my time ; but heard every opinion with fubmiffive filence, profeffed myfelf ready to learn from all who feemed inclined to teach me, paid the fame grateful acknowledgments for precepts contradictory to each other, and if any controverfy arofe, was careful to fide with her who prefided in the company.

OF this compliance I very early found the advantage ; for my aunt MATILDA left me a very large addition to my fortune, for this reafon chiefly, as fhe herfelf declared, becaufe I was not above hearing good counfel, but would fit from morning till night to be inftructed, while my fifter SUKEY, who was a year younger than myfelf, and was, therefore, in greater want of information, was fo much conceited of her own knowledge, that whenever the good lady in the ardour of benevolence reproved or inftructed her, fhe would pout or titter, interrupt her with queftions, or embarrafs her with objections.

I HAD no defign to fupplant my fifter by this complaifant attention ; nor, when the confequence

quence of my obfequioufnefs came to be known, did SUKEY fo much envy as defpife me : I was, however, very well pleafed with my fuccefs ; and having received, from the concurrent opinion of all mankind, a notion, that to be rich was to be great and happy, I thought I had obtained my advantages at an eafy rate, and refolved to continue the fame paffive attention, fince I found myfelf fo powerfully recommended by it to kindnefs and efteem.

THE defire of advifing has a very extenfive prevalence ; and fince advice cannot be given but to thofe that will hear it, a patient liftener is neceffary to the accommodation of all thofe who defire to be confirmed in the opinion of their own wifdom : a patient liftener, however, is not always to be had ; the prefent age, whatever age is prefent, is fo vitiated and difordered, that young people are readier to talk than to attend, and good counfel is only thrown away upon thofe who are full of their own perfections.

I WAS, therefore, in this fcarcity of good fenfe, a general favourite ; and feldom faw a day in which fome fober matron did not invite me to her houfe, or take me out in her chariot, for the fake of inftructing me how to keep my character in this cenforious age, how to conduct myfelf in the time of courtfhip, how to ftipulate for a fet-

tlement,

tlement, how to manage a hufband of every character, regulate my family, and educate my children.

WE are all naturally credulous in our own favour. Having been fo often careffed and applauded for my docility, I was willing to believe myfelf really enlightened by inftruction, and completely qualified for the tafk of life. I did not doubt but I was entering the world with a mind furnifhed againft all exigencies, with expedients to extricate myfelf from every difficulty, and fagacity to provide againft every danger; I was, therefore, in hafte to give fome fpecimen of my prudence, and to fhew that this liberality of inftruction had not been idly lavifhed upon a mind incapable of improvement.

My purpofe, for why fhould I deny it? was like that of other women, to obtain a hufband of rank and fortune fuperior to my own; and in this I had the concurrence of all thofe that had affumed the province of directing me. That the woman was undone who married below herfelf, was univerfally agreed: and though fome ventured to affert, that the richer man ought invariably to be preferred, and that money was a fufficient compenfation for a defective anceftry; yet the majority declared warmly for a gentleman, and were of opinion that upftarts fhould not be encouraged.

WITH

WITH regard to other qualifications I had an irreconcileable variety of inftructions. I was fometimes told, that deformity was no defect in a man; and that he who was not encouraged to intrigue by an opinion of his perfon, was more likely to value the tendernefs of his wife: but a grave widow directed me to chufe a man who might imagine himfelf agreeable to me, for that the deformed were always infupportably vigilant, and apt to fink into fullennefs, or burft into rage, if they found their wife's eye wandering for a moment to a good face or a handfome fhape.

THEY were, however, all unanimous in warning me, with repeated cautions, againft all thoughts of union with a wit, as a being with whom no happinefs could poffibly be enjoyed: men of every other kind I was taught to govern, but a wit was an animal for whom no arts of taming had been yet difcovered: the woman whom he could once get within his power, was confidered as loft to all hope of dominion or of quiet: for he would detect artifice and defeat allurement; and if once he difcovered any failure of conduct, would believe his own eyes, in defiance of tears, careffes, and proteftations.

IN purfuance of thefe fage principles, I proceeded to form my fchemes; and while I was yet in the firft bloom of youth, was taken out at an affembly by Mr. FRISK. I am afraid my

cheeks

cheeks glowed, and my eyes fparkled; for I obferved the looks of all my fuperintendants fixed anxioufly upon me; and I was next day cautioned againft him from all hands, as a man of the moft dangerous and formidable kind, who had writ verfes to one lady, and then forfaken her only becaufe fhe could not read them, and had lampooned another for no other fault than defaming his fifter.

HAVING been hitherto accuftomed to obey, I ventured to difmifs Mr. FRISK, who happily did not think me worth the labour of a lampoon. I was then addreffed by Mr. STURDY, and congratulated by all my friends on the manors of which I was fhortly to be lady: but STURDY's converfation was fo grofs, that after the third vifit I could endure him no longer; and incurred, by difmiffing him, the cenfure of all my friends, who declared that my nicety was greater than my prudence, and that they feared it would be my fate at laft to be wretched with a wit.

BY a wit, however, I was never afterwards attacked, but lovers of every other clafs, or pretended lovers, I have often had; and, notwithftanding the advice conftantly given me, to have no regard in my choice to my own inclinations, I could not forbear to difcard fome for vice, and fome for rudenefs. I was once loudly cenfured for refufing an old gentleman who offered an

enormous

enormous jointure, and died of the phthyſic a year after; and was ſo baited with inceſſant importunities, that I ſhould have given my hand to DRONE the ſtock-jobber, had not the reduction of intereſt made him afraid of the expences of matrimony.

SOME, indeed, I was permitted to encourage; but miſcarried of the main end, by treating them according to the rules of art which had been preſcribed me. ALTILIS, an old maid, infuſed into me ſo much haughtineſs and reſerve, that ſome of my lovers withdrew themſelves from my frown, and returned no more; others were driven away, by the demands of ſettlement which the widow TRAPLAND directed me to make; and I have learned, by many experiments, that to aſk advice is to loſe opportunity.

I am, S I R,

Your humble ſervant,

PERDITA

NUMB. 75.  TUESDAY, *July* 24, 1753.

——*Quid virtus & quid sapientia possit,*
*Utile proposuit nobis exemplar Ulyssem.*    HOR.

To shew what pious wisdom's pow'r can do,
The poet sets Ulysses in our view.

FRANCIS.

I HAVE frequently wondered at the common
practice of our instructors of youth, in making
their pupils far more intimately acquainted with
the ILIAD than with the ODYSSEY of HOMER.
This absurd custom, which seems to arise from
the supposed superiority of the former poem, has
inclined me to make some reflections on the
excellence of the latter; a task I am the more
readily induced to undertake, as so little is performed in the dissertation prefixed by Broome
to POPE's translation of this work, which one
may venture to pronounce is confused, defective,
and dull.   Those who receive all their opinions
in criticism from custom and authority, and never
dare to consult the decisions of reason and the
voice of nature and truth, must not accuse me of
being affectedly paradoxical, if I endeavour to
maintain that the ODYSSEY excels the ILIAD in
many respects; and that for several reasons
young

young fcholars fhould perufe it early and attentively.

THE moral of this poem is more extenfively
ufeful than that of the ILIAD ; which, indeed,
by difplaying the dire effeéts of difcord among
rulers, may rectify the conduct of princes, and
may be called the MANUAL OF MONARCHS:
whereas the patience, the prudence, the wifdom,
the temperance and fortitude of ULYSSES, afford
a pattern, the utility of which is not confined
within the compafs of courts and palaces, but
defcends and diffufes its influence over common
life and daily practice.   If the faireft examples
ought to be placed before us in an age prone to
imitation, if patriotifm be preferable to implaca-
bility, if an eager defire to return to one's country and family be more manly and noble than
an eager defire to be revenged of an enemy, then
fhould our eyes rather be fixed on ULYSSES than
ACHILLES.   Unexperienced minds, too eafily
captivated with the fire and fury of a gallant general, are apt to prefer courage to conftancy,
and firmnefs to humanity.   We do not behold
the deftroyers of peace and the murderers of
mankind, with the deteftation due to their
crimes ; becaufe we have been inured almoft
from our infancy to liften to the praifes that have
been wantonly lavifhed on them by the moft exquifite poetry : " The Mufes," to apply the
                                                    words

words of an ancient Lyric, " have concealed
" and decorated the bloody fword with wreaths
" of myrtle." Let the ILIAD be ever ranked at the
head of human compofitions for its fpirit and fublimity; but let not the milder, and, perhaps, more
infinuating and attractive beauties of the ODYS-
SEY be defpifed and overlooked. In the one we are
placed amidft the rage of ftorms and tempefts:

Ὡς δ᾽ ὑπὸ λαίλαπι πᾶσα κιλαινὴ βέβριθι χθὼν
Ἤματ᾽ ὀπωρινῷ, ὅτι λαβρότατον χέει ὕδωρ
Ζεύς, ὅτι δή ῥ᾽ ἄνδρισσι κοτισσάμενο χαλιπήνι.

Iliad XVI. 384.

And when in autumn Jove his fury pours,
And earth is loaden with inceffant fhowers:
From their deep beds he bids the rivers rife,
And opens all the flood-gates of the fkies.

POPE.

In the other, all is tranquil and fedate, and
calmly delightful:

———— Οὐτὶ ποτ᾽ ὄμβρο,
Ἀλλ᾽ αἰεὶ Ζεφύροιο λιγυπνείοντας ἀήτας
Ὠκεανὸς ἀνίησιν ἀναψύχειν ἀνθρώπους.   Odyff. IV. 566.

Stern winter fmiles on that aufpicious clime;
The fields are florid with unfading prime:
From the bleak pole no winds inclement blow,
Mold the round hail, or fhake the fleecy fnow:
But from the breezy deep, the Bleft inhale
The fragrant murmurs of the weftern gale.

POPE.

Accordingly, to diſtinguiſh the very different natures of theſe poems, it was anciently the practice of thoſe who publickly recited them, to repreſent the ILIAD, in alluſion to the bloodſhed it deſcribed, in a robe of ſcarlet; and the ODYSSEY, on account of the voyages it relates, in an azure veſtment.

THE predominant paſſion of ULYSSES being the love of his country, for the ſake of which he even refuſes immortality, the poet has taken every occaſion to diſplay it in the livelieſt and moſt ſtriking colours. The firſt time we behold the hero, we find him diſconſolately ſitting on the ſolitary ſhore, ſighing to return to Ithaca, Νόσον ἰδυεσμένων, weeping inceſſantly, and ſtill caſting his eyes upon the ſea,

Πόντον ἐπ᾽ ἀτρύγετον δερκέσκετο, δάκρυα λείβων.

" While a goddeſs," ſays Minerva at the very beginning of the poem, " by her power and her al-
" lurements detains him from Ithaca, he is dying
" with deſire to ſee even ſo much as the ſmoke
" ariſe from his much-loved iſland : tarda fluunt
" ingrataque tempora!" While the luxurious Phæacians were enjoying a delicious banquet, he attended not to their mirth and muſic, for the time approached when he was to return to Ithaca : they had prepared a ſhip for him to ſet ſail in the

very

very next morning; and the thoughts of his approaching happineſs having engroſſed all his ſoul,

He ſate, and ey'd the ſun, and wiſh'd the
    night————                    ⁀

————————Δὴ γὰρ μινίαιν νίσθαι.

To repreſent his impatience more ſtrongly, the poet adds a moſt expreſſive ſimile, ſuited to the ſimplicity of ancient times: " The ſetting of the " ſun," ſays he, " was as welcome and grateful to " ULYSSES, as it is to a well-laboured plowman, " who earneſtly waits for its decline, that he " may return to his ſupper, Δόρπου ἐποίχεσθαι, " while his weary knees are painful to him as he " walks along."

————————Βλάζιται δὶ τὰ γύνατ᾽ ἰόντι.

" Notwithſtanding all the pleaſures and endear- " ments I received from Calypſo, yet," ſays our hero, " I perpetually bedewed with my tears the " garments which this immortal beauty gave to " me."

————————Εἵματα δ' αἰεὶ
Δάκρυσι δινῖσκον τὰ μὲι ἄμβροτα δῶκι Καλυφᾶ.

                                We

We are presented in every page with fresh instances of this love of his country; and his
whole behaviour convinces us,

'Ως ἐδὺ γλύκιον ἧς παρίδος ὀλὲ τακίων.

This generous sentiment runs like a golden vein
throughout the whole poem.

IF this animating example were duly and
deeply inculcated, how strong an impression
would it necessarily make upon the yielding
minds of youth, when melted and mollified by
the warmth of such exalted poetry!

NOR is the ODYSSEY less excellent and useful,
in the amiable pictures it affords of private
affections and domestic tendernesses,

————and all the charities
Of father, son, and brother————
                                        MILTON.

WHEN ULYSSES descends into the infernal regions, it is finely contrived that he should meet
his aged mother ANTICLEA. After his first sorrow and surprize, he eagerly enquires into the
causes of her death, and adds, " Doth my fa-
" ther yet live? does my son possess my domi-
" nions, or does he groan under the tyranny of
" some usurper who thinks I shall never return?
                                        " Is

" Is my wife still conftant to my bed ? or hath
" fome noble Grecian married her ?"—Thefe
queftions are the very voice of nature and affection.    ANTICLEA anfwers, that " fhe herfelf
" died with grief for the lofs of ULYSSES ; that
" LAERTES languifhes away life in folitude and
" forrow for him ; and that PENELOPE perpe-
" tually and inconfolably bewails his abfence,
" and fighs for his return."

WHEN the hero, difguifed like a ftranger, has
the firft interview with his father, whom he finds
diverting his cares with rural amufements in his
little garden, he informs him that he had feen
his fon on his travels, but now defpairs of beholding him again. Upon this the forrow of LA-
ERTES is inexpreffible : ULYSSES can counter-
feit no longer, but exclaims ardently,

> I, I am he ! O father rife ! behold
> Thy fon !———

And the difcovery of himfelf to TELEMACHUS,
in the fixteenth book, in a fpeech of fhort and
broken exclamations, is equally tender and pathetic.

THE duties of univerfal benevolence, of charity, and of hofpitality, that unknown and un-
practifed virtue, are perpetually inculcated with
more emphafis and elegance than in any ancient
philofopher, and I wifh I could not add than in
                                                    any

any modern. ULYSSES meets with a friendly reception in all the various nations to which he is driven ; who declare their inviolable obligations to protect and cherish the stranger and the wanderer. Above all, how amiable is the behaviour of EUMEUS to his unknown master, who asks for his charity. " It is not lawful for me," says the Διὸς Ύφορϐος, " I dare not despise any " stranger or indigent man, even if he were " much meaner than thou appearest to be ; for " the poor and strangers are sent to us by JUPI- " TER !" " Keep," says EPICTETUS, " conti- " nually in thy memory, what EUMEUS speaks " in HOMER to the disguised ULYSSES." I am sensible, that many superficial French critics have endeavoured to ridicule all that passes at the lodge of EUMEUS, as coarse and indelicate, and below the dignity of Epic poetry : but let them attend to the following observation of the greatest genius of their nation : " Since it is delightful," says FENELON, " to see in one of TITIAN's land- " scapes the goats climbing up a hanging rock, or " to behold in one of TENIER's pieces a coun- " try feast and rustic dances ; it is no wonder, " that we are pleased with such natural descripti_ " ons as we find in the ODYSSEY. This simplici- " ty of manners seems to recall the golden age. " I am more pleased with honest EUMEUS, than " with the polite heroes of Clelia or Cleopatra."

THE

THE moral precepts with which every page of the ODYSSEY is pregnant, are equally noble. PLATO's wiſh is here accompliſhed ; for we behold VIRTUE perſonally appearing to the ſons of men, in her moſt awful and moſt alluring charms.

THE remaining reaſons, why the ODYSSEY is equal, if not ſuperior to the ILIAD, and why it is a poem moſt peculiarly proper for the peruſal of youth, are ; becauſe the great variety of events and ſcenes it contains, intereſt and engage the attention more than the ILIAD; becauſe characters and images drawn from familiar life, are more uſeful to the generality of readers, and are alſo more difficult to be drawn ; and becauſe the conduct of this poem, conſidered as the moſt perfect of Epopees, is more artful and judicious than that of the other.   The diſcuſſion of theſe beauties will make the ſubject of ſome enſuing paper.

Z.

NUMB. 76.   SATURDAY, *July* 28, 1753.

*Duc me*, PARENS, *celſique dominator poli,*
*Quocunque placuit ; nulla parendi mora eſt ;*
*Adſum impiger.   Fac nolle ; comitabor gemens,*
*Maluſque patiar, quod bono licuit pati.*
                              SENECA *ex* CLEANTHE(

Conduct me, thou of beings cauſe divine,
Where'er I'm deſtin'd in thy great deſign !
Active, I follow on : for ſhould my will
Reſiſt, I'm impious ; but muſt follow ſtill.
                              HARRIS.

BOZALDAB, Caliph of Egypt, had dwelt
ſecurely for many years in the ſilken pavi-
lions of pleaſure, and had every morning anointed
his head with the oil of gladneſs, when his only
ſon ABORAM, for whom he had crowded his
treaſuries with gold, extended his dominions
with conqueſts, and ſecured them with impreg-
nable fortreſſes, was ſuddenly wounded, as he
was hunting, with an arrow from an unknown
hand, and expired in the field.

BOZALDAB, in the diſtraction of grief and deſpair, refuſed to return to his palace, and retired to
the gloomieſt grotto in the neighbouring mountain : he there rolled himſelf on the duſt, tore
away the hairs of his hoary beard, and daſhed
                                        the

the cup of confolation that Patience offered him to the ground. He fuffered not his minftrels to approach his prefence ; but liftened to the fcreams of the melancholy birds of midnight, that flirt through the folitary vaults and echoing chambers of the Pyramids. "Can that GOD "be benevolent," he cried, "who thus wounds "the foul, as from an ambufh, with unexpected "forrows, and crufhes his creatures in a mo- "ment with irremediable calamity? Ye lying "Imans, prate to us no more of the juftice and "the kindnefs of an all-directing and all-loving "PROVIDENCE! HE, whom ye pretend reigns "in heaven, is fo far from protecting the mifer- "able fons of men, that he perpetually delights "to blaft the fweeteft flowerets in the garden of "HOPE; and, like a malignant giant, to beat "down the ftrongeft towers of HAPPINESS with "the iron mace of his anger. If this Being "poffeffed the goodnefs and the power with "which flattering priefts have invefted him, he "would doubtlefs be inclined, and enabled to "banifh thofe evils which render the world a "dungeon of diftrefs, a vale of vanity and woe. "—I will continue in it no longer!"

AT that moment he furioufly raifed his hand, which DESPAIR had armed with a dagger, to ftrike deep into his bofom ; when fuddenly thick flafhes of lightning fhot through the cavern, and

a be-a being of more than human beauty and magnitude, arrayed in azure robes, crowned with amaranth, and waving a branch of palm in his right hand, arrested the arm of the trembling and astonished CALIPH, and said with a majestic smile, "Follow me to the top of this mountain."

"Look from hence," said the awful conductor; "I am CALOC, the Angel of PEACE; "Look from hence into the valley."

BOZALDAB opened his eyes and beheld a barren, a sultry, and solitary island, in the midst of which sat a pale, meagre, and ghastly figure: it was a merchant just perishing with famine, and lamenting that he could find neither wild berries nor a single spring in this forlorn uninhabited desert; and begging the protection of heaven against the tigers that would now certainly destroy him, since he had consumed the last fuel he had collected to make nightly fires to affright them. He then cast a casket of jewels on the sand, as trifles of no use; and crept, feeble and trembling, to an eminence, where he was accustomed to sit every evening to watch the setting sun, and to give a signal to any ship that might haply approach the island.

"INHABITANT of heaven," cried BOZALDAB, "suffer not this wretch to perish by the fury "of wild beasts." "Peace," said the ANGEL, "and observe."

HE

HE looked again, and behold a veffel arrived at the defolate ifle. What words can paint the rapture of the ftarving merchant, when the captain offered to tranfport him to his native country, if he would reward him with half the jewels of his cafket? No fooner had this pitylefs commander received the ftipulated fum, than he held a confultation with his crew, and they agreed to feize the remaining jewels, and leave the unhappy exile in the fame helplefs and lamentable condition in which they difcovered him. He wept and trembled, intreated and implored in vain.

"WILL HEAVEN permit fuch injuftice to be "practifed," exclaimed BOZALDAB?—"Look "again," faid the ANGEL, "and behold the "very fhip in which, fhort-fighted as thou art, "thou wifhedft the merchant might embark, "dafhed in pieces on a rock: doft thou not "hear the cries of the finking failors? Prefume "not to direct the GOVERNOR of the UNIVERSE "in his difpofal of events. The man whom "thou haft pitied fhall be taken from this dreary "folitude, but not by the method thou wouldft "prefcribe. His vice was avarice, by which he "became not only abominable, but wretched; "he fancied fome mighty charm in wealth, "which, like the wand of ABDIEL, would gra-
"tify

" tify every wifh and obviate every fear.    This
" wealth he has now been taught not only to
" defpife but abhor : he cafts his jewels upon the
" fand, and confeffed them to be ufelefs ; he
" offered part of them to the mariners, and per-
" ceived them to be pernicious : he has now
" learnt, that they are rendered ufeful or vain,
" good or evil, only by the fituation and tem-
" per of the poffeffor.    Happy is he whom dif-
" trefs has taught wifdom !    But turn thine eyes
" to another and more interefting fcene."

THE CALIPH inftantly beheld a magnificent
palace, adorned with the ftatues of his anceftors
wrought in jafper ; the ivory doors of which,
turning on hinges of the gold of Golconda, difcovered a throne of diamonds, furrounded with
the RAJAS of fifty nations, and with ambaffadors
in various habits, and of different complexions ;
on which fat ABORAM, the much-lamented fon
of BOZALDAB, and by his fide a princefs fairer
than a HOURI.

" GRACIOUS ALLA !—it is my fon," cried
the CALIPH—" O let me hold him to my
" heart !" " Thou canft not grafp an unfub-
" ftantial vifion," replied the ANGEL : " I am
" now fhewing thee what would have been the
" deftiny of thy fon, had he continued longer
" on the earth."    " And why," returned Bo-
ZALDAB, " was he not permitted to con-
VOL. III.    D    " tinue ?

" tinue ? Why was I not fuffered to be a wit-
" nefs of fo much felicity and power ?"   " Con-
" fider the fequel," replied he that dwells in the
fifth heaven.   BOZALDAB looked earneftly, and
faw the countenance of his fon, on which he had
been ufed to behold the placid fmile of fimplicity
and the vivid blufhes of health, now diftorted
with rage, and now fixed in the infenfibility of
drunkennefs: it was again animated with difdain,
it became pale with apprehenfion, and appeared
to be withered by intemperance; his hands were
ftained with blood, and he trembled by turns
with fury and terror : the palace fo lately fhining
with oriental pomp, changed fuddenly into the
cell of a dungeon, where his fon lay ftretched
out on the cold pavement, gagged and bound,
with his eyes put out.   Soon after he perceived
the favourite Sultana, who before was feated by
his fide, enter with a bowl of poifon, which fhe
compelled ABORAM to drink, and afterwards
married the fucceffor to his throne.

" HAPPY," faid CALOC, " is he whom PRO-
" VIDENCE has by the angel of death fnatched
" from guilt ! from whom that power is with-
" held, which, if he had poffeffed, would have
" accumulated upon himfelf yet greater mifery
" than it could bring upon others."

" IT is enough," cried BOZALDAB; " I
" adore the infcrutable fchemes of OMNI-
" SCIENCE !—

" science !——From what dreadful evil has
" my son been refcued by a death, which I
" rafhly bewailed as unfortunate and premature ;
" a death of innocence and peace, which has
" bleffed his memory upon earth, and tranf-
" mitted his fpirit to the fkies !"

" Cast away the dagger," replied the hea-
venly meffenger, " which thou waft preparing
" to plunge into thine own heart.  Exchange
" complaint for filence, and doubt for adora-
" tion.  Can a mortal look down, without gid-
" dinefs and ftupefaction, into the vaft abyfs
" of Eternal Wisdom ?  Can a mind that
" fees not infinitely, perfectly comprehend any
" thing among an infinity of objects mutually
" relative ?  Can the channels, which thou
" commandeft to be cut to receive the annual
" inundations of the Nile, contain the waters
" of the Ocean ?  Remember, that perfect hap-
" pinefs cannot be conferred on a creature ; for
" perfect happinefs is an attribute as incommu-
" nicable as perfect power and eternity."

The Angel, while he was fpeaking thus,
ftretched out his pinions to fly back to the Em-
pyreum ; and the flutter of his wings was like
the rufhing of a cataract.

Z

NUMB. 77. TUESDAY, *July* 31, 1753.

———*Peccare docentes*
*Fallax hiſtorias monet.*                          HOR.

To tint th' attentive mind ſhe tries
With tales of exemplary vice.

## To the ADVENTURER.

SIR,

I SHALL make no apology for the trouble I am about to give you, ſince I am ſure the motives that induce me to give it, will have as much weight with you as they have with me : I ſhall therefore, without further preface, relate to you the events of a life, which, however inſignificant and unentertaining, affords a leſſon of the higheſt importance ; a leſſon, the value of which I have experienced, and may, therefore, recommend.

I AM the daughter of a gentleman of good family, who, as he was a younger brother, purchaſed with the portion that was allotted him, a genteel poſt under the government. My mother died when I was but twelve years old ; and my father, who was exceſſively fond of me, determined to be himſelf my preceptor, and to take care that my natural genius, which his partiality made him think above the common rank, ſhould

not

not want the improvements of a liberal education.

He was a man of sense, with a tolerable share of learning. In his youth he had been a free-liver, and perhaps for that reason took some pains to become what is called a free-thinker. But whatever fashionable frailties he might formerly have allowed in himself, he was now in advanced life, and had at least worldly wisdom enough to know, that it was necessary his daughter should be restrained from those liberties, which he had looked upon as trifling errors in his own conduct. He, therefore, laboured with great application to inculcate in me the love of order, the beauty of moral rectitude, and the happiness and self-reward of virtue; but at the same time professed it his design to free my mind from vulgar prejudices and superstition, for so he called REVEALED RELIGION. As I was urged to chuse virtue, and reject vice, from motives which had no necessary connection with immortality, I was not led to consider a future state either with hope or fear: my father indeed, when I urged him upon that subject, always intimated that the doctrine of immortality, whether true or false, ought not at all to influence my conduct or interrupt my peace; because the virtue which secured happiness in the present state, would also secure it in a future: a future state, therefore, I wholly disregarded, and, to confess a truth, disbelieved:

for

for I thought I could plainly difcover that it was
difbelieved by my father, though he had not
thought fit explicitly to declare his fentiments.
As I had no very turbulent paffions, a ductile
and good difpofition, and the higheft reverence
for his underftanding, as well as the tendereft
affection for him, he found it an eafy tafk to
make me adopt every fentiment and opinion
which he propofed to me as his own ; efpecially,
as he took care to fupport his principles by the
authority and arguments of the beft writers
againft CHRISTIANITY. At the age of twenty
I was called upon to make ufe of all the philofophy I had been taught, by his death ; which
not only deprived me of a parent I moft ardently
loved, but with him of all the eafe and affluence
to which I had been accuftomed. His income
was only for life, and he had rather lived beyond than within it ; confequently, there was
nothing left for me but the pride and helpleffnefs
of genteel life, a tafte for every thing elegant,
and a delicacy and fenfibility that has doubled all
my fufferings. In this diftrefs a brother of my
mother's, who was grown rich in trade, received
me into his houfe, and declared he would take
the fame care of me as if I had been his own
child. When the firft tranfports of my grief
were abated, I found myfelf in an eafy fituation,
and from the natural chcerfulnefs of my temper,

I was

I was beginning once more to taste of happiness.
My uncle, who was a man of a narrow understanding and illiberal education, was a little dif-
gusted with me for employing so much of my
time in reading ; but still more so, when, hap-
pening to examine my books, he found by the
titles that some of them were what he called
blasphemy, and tended, as he imagined, to make
me an Atheist.  I endeavoured to explain my
principles, which I thought it beneath the dignity of virtue to disguise or disavow ; but as I
never could make him conceive any difference
between a Deist and an Atheist, my arguments
only served to confirm him in the opinion that I
was a wicked wretch, who, in his own phrase,
believed neither God nor Devil.  As he was
really a good man, and heartily zealous for the
established faith, though more from habit and
prejudice than reason, my errors gave him great
affliction : I perceived it with the utmost concern ; I perceived too, that he looked upon me
with a degree of abhorrence mixed with pity,
and that I was wholly indebted to his good-na-
ture for that protection which I had flattered
myself I should owe to his love.  I comforted
myself, however, with my own integrity, and
even felt a conscious pride in suffering this per-
secution from ignorance and folly, only because
I was superior to vulgar errors and popular superstition ;

perftition; and that CHRISTIANITY deferved
thefe appellations, I was not more convinced by
my father's arguments than my uncle's conduct,
who, as his zeal was not according to knowledge, was by no means qualified to " adorn the
" doctrine which he profeffed to believe."

I HAD lived a few months under the painful
fenfibility of receiving continual benefits from a
perfon whofe efteem and affection I had loft,
when my uncle one day came into my chamber,
and after preparing me for fome unexpected good
fortune, told me, he had juft had a propofal of
marriage for me from a man to whom I could
not poffibly have any objection. He then named
a merchant, with whom I had often been in company at his table. As the man was neither old
nor ugly, had a large fortune and a fair character,
my uncle thought himfelf fufficiently authorifed
to pronounce as he did, that I could not poffibly
have any objection to him. An objection, however, I had, which I told my uncle was to me
infuperable; it was, that the perfon whom he
propofed to me as the companion, the guide and
director of my whole life, to whom I was to vow
not only obedience but love, had nothing in him
that could ever engage my affection : his underftanding was low, his fentiments mean and indelicate, and his manner unpolite and unpleafing.
——" What ftuff is all this," interrupted my
uncle,

uncle, "fentiments indelicate! unpolite! his
"underftanding, forfooth, not equal to your
"own! Ah, child, if you had lefs romance,
"conceit and arrogance, and more true difcre-
"tion and prudence, it would do you more good
"than all the fine books you have confounded
"your poor head with, and what is worfe, per-
"haps, ruined your poor foul. I own, it went
"a little againft my confcience to acccept my
"honeft friend's kind offer, and give him fuch
"a pagan for his wife. But how know I whe-
"ther the believing hufband may not convert
"the unbelieving wife?——As to your flighty
"objections, they are fuch nonfenfe, that I
"wonder you can fuppofe me fool enough to be
"deceived by them. No, child; wife as you are,
"you cannot impofe upon a man who has lived
"as many years in the world as I have. I fee
"your motive; you have fome infidel libertine
"rake in your eye, with whom you would go
"headlong to perdition. But I fhall take care
"not to have your foul to anfwer for as well as
"your perfon. Either I fhall difpofe of you to
"an houeft man that may convert you, or you
"fhall difpofe of yourfelf how you pleafe for
"me; for I difclaim all further care or trouble
"about you: fo I leave you to confider, whether
"or no the kindnefs I have fhewn you, entitles
"me to fome little influence over you, and

D 5 "whether.

" whether you chuse to seek protection where
" you can find it, or accept of the happy lot
" providence has cut out for you."

HE left me at the close of this fine harangue,
and I seriously set myself to consider as he bade
me, which of the two states he had set before
me I ought to chuse; to submit to a legal sort of
prostitution, with the additional weight of per-
jury on my conscience, or to expose myself to
all the distresses of friendless poverty, and un-
protected youth. After some hours of deliberation, I determined on the latter, and that more
from principle than inclination; for though my
delicacy would have suffered extremely in accepting a husband, at least indifferent to me;
yet as my heart was perfectly disengaged, and
my temper naturally easy, I thought I could have
been less unhappy in following my uncle's advice, than I might probably be by rejecting it:
but then I must have submitted to an action I
could not think justifiable, in order to avoid mere
external distresses. This would not have been
philosophical. I had always been taught, that
virtue was of itself sufficient to happiness; and
that those things which are generally esteemed
evils, could have no power to disturb the felicity
of a mind governed by the eternal rule of right,
and truly enamoured of the charms of moral
beauty. I resolved, therefore, to run all risques,
                                          rather

rather than depart from this glorious principle;
I felt myself raised by the trial, and exulted in
the opportunity of shewing my contempt of the
smiles or frowns of fortune, and of proving the
power of virtue to sustain the soul under all accidental circumstances of distress.

I COMMUNICATED my resolution to my uncle,
assuring him at the same time of my everlasting
gratitude and respect, and that nothing should
have induced me to offend or disobey him, but
his requiring me to do what my reason and conscience disapproved; that supposing the advantages of riches to be really as great as he
believed, yet still those of virtue were greater,
and I could not resolve to purchase the one by
a violation of the other; that a false vow was
certainly criminal; and that it would be doing
an act of the highest injustice, to enter into so
solemn an engagement without the power of
fulfilling it; that my affections did not depend
on my own will; and that no man should possess my person, who could not obtain the first
place in my heart.

I WAS surprised that my uncle's impatience
had permitted me to go on thus far; but looking
in his face, I perceived that passion had kept him
silent. At length the gathering storm burst over
my head in a torrent of reproaches. My reasons
were condemned as romantic absurdities, which

D 6          I could

I could not myself believe; I was accused of
designing to deceive, and to throw myself away
on some worthless fellow, whose principles were
as bad as my own.    It was in vain for me to
assert that I had no such design, nor any inclination to marry at all; my uncle could sooner
have believed the grosseft contradiction, than that
a young woman could so strenuously refuse one
man without being prepoffeffed in favour of another.    As I thought myself injured by his ac-
cufations and tyranny, I gave over the attempt to
mitigate his anger.    He appealed to Heaven for
the juftice of his refentment, and againft my ingratitude and rebellion; and then giving me a
note of fifty pounds, which he said would keep me
from immediate indigence, he bade me leave his
houfe, and fee his face no more.    I bowed in
fign of obedience; and collecting all my dignity
and refolution, I arofe, thanked him for his paft
benefits, and with a low curt'fy left the room.

    In lefs than an hour I departed with my little
wardrobe to the houfe of a perfon who had formerly been my father's fervant, and who now kept
a fhop and let lodgings.    From hence I went the
next day to vifit my father's nephew, who was in
poffeffion of the family eftate, and had lately married a lady of great fortune.    He was a young
gentleman of good parts, his principles the
fame as my father's, though his practice had not
                                                    been

been quite agreeable to the ſtrict rules of morality: however, ſetting aſide a few of thoſe vices
which are looked upon as genteel accompliſhments in young fellows of fortune, I thought
him a good ſort of man; and as we had always
lived in great kindneſs, I doubted not that I
ſhould find him my friend, and meet with approbation and encouragement at leaſt, if not aſſiſtance from him. I told him my ſtory, and the
reaſons that had determined me to the refuſal
that had incurred my uncle's diſpleaſure. But
how was I diſappointed, when, inſtead of the
applauſe I expected for my heroic virtue and un-
merited perſecutions, I perceived a ſmile of contempt on his face, when he interrupted me in
the following manner: " And what, in the
" devil's name, my dear couſin, could make a
" woman of your ſenſe behave ſo like an idiot:
" What! forfeit all your hopes from your uncle,
" refuſe an excellent match, and reduce your-
" ſelf to beggary, becauſe truly you were not in
" love? Surely, one might have expected better
" from you even at fifteen. Who is it pray
" that marries the perſon of their choice? For
" my own part, who have rather a better title
" to pleaſe myſelf with a good fifteen hundred
" a-year, than you who have not a ſhilling, I
" found it would not do, and that there was
" ſomething more to be ſought after in a wife
                                    " than

" than a pretty face or a genius ? Do you think
" I cared three farthings for the woman I mar-
" ried ? No, faith.   But her thirty thoufand
" pounds were worth having; with that I can
" purchafe a feraglio of beauties, and indulge
" my tafte in every kind of pleafure.   And pray
" what is it to me whether my wife has beauty,
" or wit, or elegance, when her money will
" fupply me with all that in others ? You,
" coufin, had an opportunity of being as happy
" as I am : the men, believe me, would not like
" you a bit the worfe for being married ; on the
" contrary, you would find, that for one who
" took notice of you as a fingle woman, twenty
" would be your admirers and humble fervants. .
" when there was no danger of being taken-in.
" Thus you might have gratified all your paf-
" fions, made an elegant figure in life, and have
" chofen out fome gentle fwain as romantic and
" poetical as you pleafed for your Cecifbee.
" The good John Trot hufband would have
" been eafily managed, and——" Here my
indignation could be contained no longer, and I
was leaving the room in difdain, when he caught
me by the hand—" Nay, prithee, my dear coufin,
" none of thefe violent airs.   I thought you and
" I had known one another better.   Let the
" poor fouls, who are taught by the priefts and
" their nurfes to be afraid of hell-fire, and to
                                    " think

" think they shall go to the devil for following
" nature and making life agreeable, be as out-
" rageously virtuous as they please: you have
" too much sense to be frighted at bugbears;
" you know that the term of your existence is
" but short; and it is highly reasonable to make
" it as pleasant as possible."—I was too angry
to attempt confuting his arguments; but burst-
ing from his hold, told him I would take care
not to give him a second opportunity of insult-
ing my distress, and affronting my understanding; and so left his house with a resolution never
to enter it again.

Y

✱✱✱✱✱✱✱✱✱✱✱✱✱✱✱✱✱✱✱✱✱✱✱✱✱✱✱

NUMB. 78. SATURDAY, *August* 4, 1753.

——*Propter vitam vivendi perdere causas.*

JUV.

Nor quit for life, what gives to life its worth.

I WENT home mortified and disappointed.
My spirits sunk into a dejection, which took
from me for many days all inclination to stir out
of my lodging, or to see a human face. At
length I resolved to try, whether indigence and
friendship were really incompatible, and whether

I should

I fhould meet with the fame treatment from a female friend, whofe affection had been the principal pleafure of my youth. Surely, thought I, the gentle AMANDA, whofe heart feems capable of every tender and generous fentiment, will do juftice to the innocence and integrity of her unfortunate friend ; her tendernefs will encourage my virtue and animate my fortitude, her praifes and endearments will compenfate all my hardfhips. AMANDA was a fingle woman of a moderate independent fortune, which I heard fhe was going to beftow on a young officer, who had little or nothing befides his commiffion. I had no doubt of her approbation of my refufing a mercenary match, fince fhe herfelf had chofen from motives fo oppofite to thofe which are called prudent. She had been in the country fome months, fo that my misfortunes had not reached her ear till I myfelf related them to her. She heard me with great attention, and anfwered me with politenefs enough, but with a coldnefs that chilled my very heart. " You are fenfible, my " dear FIDELIA," faid fhe, " that I never pre- " tended to fet my underftanding in competition " with yours. I knew my own inferiority ; and " though many of your notions and opinions " appeared to me very ftrange and particular, " I never attempted to difpute them with you. " To be fure, you know beft ; but it feems to " me

" me a very odd conduct for one in your situ-
" ation to give offence to fo good an uncle;
" firft by maintaining doctrines which may be
" very true for ought I know, but which are
" very contrary to the received opinions we are
" brought up in, and therefore are apt to fhock
" a common underftanding; and fecondly, to
" renounce his protection, and throw yourfelf
" into the wide world, rather than marry the man
" he chofe for you; to whom, after all, I do
" not find you had any real objection, nor any
" antipathy for his perfon."—Antipathy, my
dear! faid I; are there not many degrees between
loving and honouring a man preferably to all
others, and beholding him with abhorrence and
averfion? The firft is, in my opinion, the duty
of a wife, a duty voluntarily taken upon herfelf,
and engaged in under the moft folemn contract.
As to the difficulties that may attend my friend-
lefs, unprovided ftate, fince they are the confequences of a virtuous action, they cannot really
be evils, nor can they difturb that happinefs
which is the gift of virtue. " I am heartily
" glad," anfwered fhe, " that you have found
" the art of making yourfelf happy by the force
" of imagination? I wifh your enthufiafm may
" continue; and that you may ftill be further
" convinced, by your own experience, of the
" folly

" folly of mankind, in fuppofing poverty and
" difgrace to be evils."

I was cut to the foul by the unkind manner
which accompanied this farcafm, and was going
to remonftrate againft her unfriendly treatment,
when her lover came in with another gentleman,
who, in fpite of my full heart, engaged my attention, and for a while made me forget the ftings
of unkindnefs. The beauty and gracefulnefs of
his perfon caught my eye, and the politenefs of
his addrefs and the elegance of his compliments
foon prejudiced me in favour of his underftanding.
He was introduced by the CAPTAIN to AMANDA
as his moft intimate friend, and feemed defirous
to give credit to his friend's judgment by making
himfelf as agreeable as poffible. He fucceeded fo
well, that AMANDA was wholly engroffed by
the pleafure of his converfation, and the care of
entertaining her lover and her new gueft; her
face brightened, and her good humour returned.
When I arofe to leave her, fhe preffed me fo
earneftly to ftay dinner, that I could not, without difcovering how much I refented her behaviour, refufe. This, however, I fhould probably have done, as I was naturally difpofed to
fhow every fentiment of my heart, had not a
fecret wifh arofe there to know a little more of
this agreeable ftranger. This inclined me to
think it prudent to conceal my refentment, and

to

to accept the civilities of AMANDA. The conversation grew more and more pleasing; I took
my share in it, and had more than my share of
the charming stranger's notice and attention. As
we all grew more and more unreserved, AMANDA
dropt hints in the course of the conversation relating to my story, my sentiments, and unhappy
situation. Sir GEORGE FREELOVE, for that
was the young gentleman's name, listened gree-
dily to all that was said of me, and seemed to
eye me with earnest curiosity as well as admiration. We did not part till it was late, and Sir
George insisted on attending me to my lodgings:
I strongly refused it, not without a sensation which
more properly belonged to the female than the
philosopher, and which I condemned in myself
as arising from dishonest pride. I could not
without pain suffer the polite Sir GEORGE, upon
so short an acquaintance, to discover the mean-
ness of my abode. To avoid this, I sent for a
chair; but was confused to find, that Sir GEORGE
and his servants prepared to attend it on foot by
way of guard; it was in vain to dispute; he
himself walked before, and his servants followed
it. I was covered with blushes, when, after all
this parade, he handed me in at the little shop
door, and took leave with as profound respect as
if he had guarded me to a palace. A thousand
different thoughts kept me from closing my eyes

that

that night. The behaviour of AMANDA wounded
me to the foul : I found that I muſt look on her
as no more than a common acquaintance ; and
that the world did not contain one perſon whom
I could call my friend.   My heart felt deſolate
and forlorn ; I knew not what courſe to take for
my future ſubſiſtence ; the pain which my pride
had juſt given me, convinced me that I was far
from having conquered the paſſions of humanity,
and that I ſhould feel too ſenſibly all the mortifi-
cations which attend on poverty.   I determined,
however, to ſubdue this pride, and called to my
aſſiſtance the examples of ancient ſages and philo-
ſophers, who deſpiſed riches and honours, and
felt no inconveniences from the malice of fortune.
I had almoſt reaſoned myſelf into a contempt for
the world, and fancied myſelf ſuperior to its
ſmiles or frowns ; when the idea of Sir GEORGE
FREELOVE ruſhed upon my mind, and deſtroyed
at once the whole force of my reaſoning.   I found
that however I might diſregard the reſt of the
world, 1 could not be indifferent to his opinion ;
and the thought of being deſpiſed by him was
inſupportable.   I recollected that my condition
was extremely different from that of an old philoſopher, whoſe rags perhaps were the means of
gratifying his pride, by attracting the notice and
reſpect of mankind : at leaſt, the philoſopher's
ſchemes and wiſhes were very different from thoſe
                                        which

which at that time were taking poffeffion of my
heart.   The looks and behaviour of Sir GEORGE
left me no doubt that I had made as deep an
impreffion in his favour, as he had done in mine.
I could not bear to lofe the ground I had gained,
and to throw myfelf into a ftate below his notice.   I fcorned the thoughts of impofing on him
with regard to my circumftances, in cafe he
fhould really have had favourable intentions for
me; yet to difgrace myfelf for ever in his eye,
by fubmitting to fervitude, or any low way of
fupporting myfelf, was what I could not bring
myfelf to refolve on.

   IN the midft of thefe reflections I was furprifed
the next morning by a vifit from Sir GEORGE.
He made refpectful apologies for the liberty he
took; told me he had learnt from my friend,
that the unkindnefs and tyranny of an uncle had
caft me into uneafy circumftances; and that he
could not know, that fo much beauty and merit
were fo unworthily treated by fortune, without
earneftly wifhing to be the inftrument of doing
me more juftice.   He entreated me to add dignity and value to his life, by making it conducive
to the happinefs of mine; and was going on with
the moft fervent offers of fervice, when I interrupted him by faying, that there was nothing in
his power that I could with honour accept, by
which my life could be made happier, but that
                    refpect

respect which was due to me as a woman and a gentlewoman, and which ought to have prevented such offers of service from a stranger, as could only be justified by a long experienced friendship; that I was not in a situation to receive visits, and must decline his acquaintance, which neverthelefs in a happier part of my life would have given me pleasure.

He now had recourse to all the arts of his sex, imputing his too great freedom to the force of his passion, protesting the most inviolable respect, and imploring on his knees, and even with tears, that I would not punish him so severely as to deny him the liberty of seeing me, and making himself more and more worthy of my esteem. My weak heart was but too much touched by his artifices, and I had only just fortitude enough to persevere in refusing his visits, and to insist on his leaving me, which at last he did; but it was after such a profusion of tenderness, prayers, and protestations, that it was some time before I could recal my reason enough to reflect on the whole of his behaviour, and on my own situation, which compared, left me but little doubt of his dishonourable views.

I determined never more to admit him to my presence, and accordingly gave orders to be denied if he came again. My reason applauded, but my heart reproached me, and heavily repined

pined at the rigid determination of prudence. I
knew that I acted rightly, and I expected that
that confcioufnefs would make me happy, but
I found it otherwife; I was wretched beyond
what I had ever felt or formed any idea of; I
difcovered that my heart was entangled in a paffion which muft for ever be combated, or indulged at the expence of virtue. I now confidered riches as truly defirable, fince they would
have placed me above difgraceful attempts, and
given me reafonable hopes of becoming the wife
of Sir GEORGE FREELOVE. I was difcontented
and unhappy, but furprifed and difappointed
to find myfelf fo, fince hitherto I had no one
criminal action to reproach myfelf with; on the
contrary, my difficulties were all owing to my
regard for virtue.

I RESOLVED, however, to try ftill farther the
power of virtue to confer happinefs, to go on in
my obedience to her laws, and patiently wait
for the good effects of it. But I had ftronger
difficulties to go through than any I had yet
experienced. Sir GEORGE was too much practifed in the arts of feduction, to be difcouraged
by a firft repulfe: every day produced either fome
new attempt to fee me, or a letter full of the
moft paffionate proteftations and entreaties for
pardon and favour. It was in vain I gave orders
that no more letters fhould be taken in from him;

he

he had fo many different contrivances to convey them, and directed them in hands fo unlike, that I was furprifed into reading them contrary to my real intentions. Every time I ftirred out he was fure to be in my way, and to employ the moft artful tongue that ever enfnared the heart of woman, in blinding my reafon and awakening my paffions.

My virtue, however, did not yet give way, but my peace of mind was utterly deftroyed. Whenever I was with him, I fummoned all my fortitude, and conftantly repeated my commands that he fhould avoid me. His difobedience called for my refentment, and, in fpite of my melting heart, I armed my eyes with anger, and treated him with as much difdain as I thought his un-worthy defigns deferved. But the moment he left me, all my refolution forfook me. I repined at my fate : I even murmured againft the Sove-reign Ruler of all things, for making me fub-ject to paffions which I could not fubdue, yet muft not indulge : I compared my own fituation with that of my libertine coufin, whofe perni-cious arguments I had heard with horror and deteftation, who gave the reins to every defire, whofe houfe was the feat of plenty, mirth, and de-light, whofe face was ever covered with fmiles, and whofe heart feemed free from forrow and care. Is not this man, faid I, happier than I am? And if fo, where is the worth of virtue?

Have

Have I not facrificed to her my fortune and my
-friends? Do I not daily facrifice to her my darling inclination? Yet what is the compenfation
fhe offers me? What are my profpects in this
world but poverty, mortification, difappointment
and grief? Every wifh of my heart denied,
every paffion of humanity combated and hurt,
though never conquered! Are thefe the bleffings
with which HEAVEN diftinguifhes its favourites?
Can the KING OF HEAVEN want power or will to
diftinguifh them? Or does he leave his wretched
creatures to be the fport of chance, the prey of
wickednefs and malice? Surely, no. Yet is
not the condition of the virtuous often more
miferable than that of the vicious? I myfelf
have experienced that it is. I am very unhappy,
and fee no likelihood of my being otherwife in
this world—and all beyond the grave is eternal
darknefs. Yet why do I fay, that I have no
profpect of happinefs? Does not the moft en-
gaging of men offer me all the joys that Jove
and fortune can beftow? Will not he protect
me from every infult of the proud world that
fcoffs at indigence? Will not his liberal hand
pour forth the means of every pleafure, even of
that higheft and trueft of all pleafures, the power
of relieving the fufferings of my fellow-crea-
tures, of changing the tears of diftrefs into tears
of joy and gratitude, of communicating my own

happineſs to all around me? Is not this a ſtate far preferable to that in which virtue has placed me? But what is virtue? Is not happineſs the laudable purſuit of reaſon? Is it not then laudable to purſue it by the moſt probable means? Have I not been accuſing PROVIDENCE of unkindneſs, whilſt I myſelf only am in fault for rejecting its offered favours? Surely, I have miſtaken the path of virtue: it muſt be that which leads to happineſs. The path which I am in, is full of thorns and briars, and terminates in impenetrable darkneſs; but I ſee another that is ſtrowed with flowers, and bright with the ſunſhine of proſperity: this, ſurely, is the path of virtue, and the road to happineſs. Hither then let me turn my weary ſteps, nor let vain and idle prejudices fright me from felicity. It is ſurely impoſſible that I ſhould offend GOD, by yielding to a temptation which he has given me no motive to reſiſt. He has allotted me a ſhort and precarious exiſtence, and has placed before me good and evil.—What is good but pleaſure? What is evil but pain? Reaſon and nature direct me to chuſe the firſt, and avoid the laſt. I ſought for happineſs in what is called virtue, but I found it not: ſhall I not try the other experiment, ſince I think I can hardly be more unhappy by following inclination, than I am by denying it?

THUS

THUS had my frail thoughts wandered into a wildernefs of error, and thus had I almoft reafoned myfelf out of every principle of morality, by purfuing through all their confequences the doctrines which had been taught me as rules of life and prefcriptions for felicity, the talifmans of TRUTH, by which I fhould be fecured in the ftorms of adverfity, and liften without danger to the fyrens of temptation ; when in the fatal hour of my prefumption, fitting alone in my chamber, collecting arguments on the fide of paffion, almoft diftracted with doubts, and plunging deeper and deeper into falfehood, I faw Sir GEORGE FREELOVE at my feet, who had gained admittance, contrary to my orders, by corrupting my landlady.   It is not neceffary to defcribe to you his arts, or the weak efforts of that virtue which had been gracioufly implanted in my heart, but which I had taken impious pains to undermine by falfe reafoning, and which now tottered from the foundation : fuffice it that I fubmitted to the humiliation I have fo well deferved, and tell you, that, in all the pride of human reafon, I dared to condemn, as the effect of weaknefs and prejudice, the ftill voice of confcience which would yet have warned me from ruin ; that my innocence, my honour, was the facrifice to paffion and fophiftry ; that my boafted philofophy, and too much flattered underftanding, preferved me not from the loweſt depth of infamy, which the weakeſt of my ſex with humility and religion would have avoided.

I NOW experienced a new kind of wretched-neſs. My vile ſeducer tried in vain to reconcile me to the ſhameful life to which he had reduced me, by loading me with finery, and laviſhing his fortune in procuring me pleaſures which I could not taſte, and pomp which ſeemed an inſult on my diſgrace. In vain did I recollect the arguments which had convinced me of the lawfulneſs of accepting offered pleaſures, and following the dictates of inclination : the light of my underſtanding was darkened, but the ſenſe of guilt was not loſt. My pride and my delicacy, if, criminal as I was, I may dare to call it ſo, ſuffered the moſt intolerable mortification and diſguſt, every time I reflected on my infamous ſituation. Every eye ſeemed to upbraid me, even that of my triumphant ſeducer. O depth of miſery ! to be conſcious of deſerving the contempt of him I loved, and for whoſe ſake I was become contemptible to myſelf.

Y

NUMB. 79. TUESDAY, *August* 7, 1753.

*Quisnam igitur liber? Sapiens: sibi qui im-*
*periosus;*
*Quem neque pauperies, neque mors, neque vin-*
*cula terrent:*
*Responsare cupidinibus, contemnere honores*
*Fortis, et in seipso totus: teres atque rotundus,*
*Externi ne quid valeat per læve morari.*

HOR.

Who then is free?—The wise, who well
maintains
An empire o'er himself: whom neither chains,
Nor want, nor death, with flavish fear in----
Who can ambition's vaineft gifts despise;
Firm in himself who on himself relies;
Polish'd and round who runs his proper course,
And breaks misfortune with superior force.

FRANCIS.

THIS was the state of my mind during a
year which I passed in Sir GEORGE's
house. His fondness was unabated for eight
months of the time; and as I had no other object to share my attention, neither friend nor rela-
tion to call off any part of my tenderness, all the
love of a heart naturally affectionate centered

E 3                                           in

in him.    The firſt dawnings of unkindneſs
were but too viſible to my watchful eyes.    I had
now all the torments of jealouſy to endure, till
a cruel certainty put an end to them.    I learnt
at length, that my falſe lover was on the brink of
marriage with a lady of great fortune.    I immediately reſolved to leave him ; but could not do
it without firſt venting my full heart in complaints and reproaches.    This provoked his rage,
and drew on me inſolence, which though I had
deſerved, I had not learnt to bear.    I returned
with ſcorn, which no longer became me, all the
wages of my ſin, and the trappings of my ſhame,
and left his houſe in the bittereſt anguiſh of
·· ······ and deſpair.

to bear a ſcene which recalled every circumſtance
of my undoing, aſhamed to look in the face of
any creature who had ſeen me innocent, wretched
in myſelf, and hoping from change of place ſome
abatement of my miſery, I put myſelf into a
poſt-chaiſe at two in the morning, with orders
to the driver to carry me as far from town as he
could before the return of night, leaving it to
him to chuſe the road.

My reaſon and my ſenſes ſeemed benumbed
and ſtupified during my journey.    I made no reflections on what I was about, nor formed any
deſign for my future life.    When night came, my

                              conductor

conductor would have ftopt at a large town, but
I bid him go on to the next village. There
I alighted at a paultry inn, and difmiffed my
vehicle, without once confidering what I was
to do with myfelf, or why I chofe that place for
my abode. To fay truth, I can give no account of my thoughts at this period of time:
they were all confufed and diftracted. A fhort
frenzy muft have filled up thofe hours, of which
my memory retains fuch imperfect traces. I remember only, that without having pulled off my
clothes, I left the inn as foon as I faw the day,
and wandered out of the village.

My unguided feet carried me to a range of
willows by a river's fide, where after having
walked fome time, the frefhnefs of the air re-
vived my fenfes, and awakened my reafon. My
reafon, my memory, my anguifh and defpair,
returned together! Every circumftance of my
paft life was prefent to my mind; but moft the
idea of my faithlefs lover and my criminal love
tortured my imagination, and rent my bleeding
heart, which, in fpite of all its guilt and all its
wrongs, retained the tendereft and moft ardent
affection for its undoer. This unguarded affection, which was the effect of a gentle and
kind nature, heightened the anguifh of refentment, and completed my mifery. In vain did I
call off my thoughts from this gloomy retro-

fpect,

fpect, and hope to find a gleam of comfort in my future profpects. They were ftill more dreadful : poverty, attended by infamy and want, groaning under the cruel hand of oppreffion and the taunts of infolence, was before my eyes. I, who had once been the darling and the pride of indulgent parents, who had once been beloved, refpected, and admired, was now the outcaft of human nature, defpifed and avoided by all who had ever loved me, by all whom I had moft loved! hateful to myfelf, belonging to no one, expofed to wrongs and infults from all!

I TRIED to find out the caufe of this difmal change, and how far I was myfelf the occafion of it. My conduct with refpect to Sir GEORGE, though I fpontaneoufly condemned, yet, upon recollection, I thought the arguments which produced it would juftify. But as my principles could not preferve me from vice, neither could they fuftain me in adverfity : confcience was not to be perverted by the fophiftry which had beclouded my reafon. And if any, by imputing my conduct to error, fhould acquit me of guilt, let them remember, it is yet true, that in this uttermoft diftrefs, I was neither fuftained by the confcioufnefs of innocence, the exultation of virtue, nor the hope of reward : whether I looked backward or forward, all was confufion

and

and anguiſh, diſtraction and deſpair. I accuſed the SUPREME BEING of cruelty and injuſtice, who, though he gave me not ſufficient encouragement to reſiſt deſire, yet puniſhed me with the conſequences of indulgence. If there is a GOD, cried I, he muſt be either tyrannical and cruel, or regardleſs of his creatures. I will no longer endure a being which is undeſervedly miſerable either from chance or deſign, but fly to that annihilation in which all my proſpects terminate. Take back, ſaid I, lifting my eyes to HEAVEN, the hateful gift of exiſtence, and let my duſt no more be animated to ſuffering, and exalted to miſery.

So ſaying, I ran to the brink of the river, and was going to plunge in, when the cry of ſome perſon very near me made me turn my eyes to ſee whence it came. I was accoſted by an elderly clergyman, who with looks of terror, pity and benevolence, aſked what I was about to do? At firſt I was ſullen, and refuſed to anſwer him; but by degrees the compaſſion he ſhowed, and the tenderneſs with which he treated me, ſoftened my heart, and gave vent to my tears.

"O! MADAM," ſaid he, "theſe are gra-
"cious ſigns, and unlike thoſe which firſt drew
"my attention, and made me watch you unob-
"ſerved, fearing ſome fatal purpoſe in your
"mind. What muſt be the thoughts which

E 5                        "could

" could make a face like your's appear the picture
" of horror ! I was taking my morning walk,
" and have feen you a confiderable time ; fome-
" times ftopping and wringing your hands,
" fometimes quickening your pace, and fome-
" times walking flow with your eyes fixed on
" the ground, till you raifed them to Heaven,
" with looks not of fupplication and piety, but
" rather of accufation and defiance.  For pity
" tell me how is it that you have quarrelled
" with yourfelf, with life, nay even with
" HEAVEN ? Recal your reafon and your hope,
" and let this feafonable prevention of your fatal
" purpofe be an earneft to you of good things
" to come, of GOD's mercy not yet alienated
" from you, and ftooping from his throne to
" fave your foul from perdition."

THE tears which flowed in rivers from my
eyes while he talked, gave me fo much relief,
that I found myfelf able to fpeak, and defirous
to exprefs my gratitude for the good man's concern for me.   It was fo long fince I had known
the joys of confidence, that I felt furprifing
pleafure and comfort from unburthening my
heart, and telling my kind deliverer every circumftance of my ftory, and every thought of
my diftracted mind.  He fhuddered to hear me
upbraid the DIVINE PROVIDENCE; and ftopping
me fhort, told me, he would lead me to one

who

who should preach patience to me, whilst she gave me the example of it.

As we talked he led me to his own house, and there introduced me to his wife, a middle-aged woman, pale and emaciated, but of a cheerful placid countenance, who received me with the greatest tenderness and humanity. She saw I was distressed, and her compassion was beforehand with my complaints. Her tears stood ready to accompany mine; her looks and her voice expressed the kindest concern; and her assiduous cares demonstrated that true politeness and hospitality, which is not the effect of art but of inward benevolence. While she obliged me to take some refreshment, her husband gave her a short account of my story, and of the state in which he had found me. "This poor lady," said he, "from the fault of her education and prin-
"ciples, sees every thing through a gloomy
"medium: she accuses PROVIDENCE, and hates
"her existence for those evils, which are the
"common lot of mankind in this short state of
"trial. You, my dear, who are one of the
"greatest sufferers I have known, are best
"qualified to cure her of her faulty impatience;
"and to convince her, by your own example,
"that this world is not the place in which Vir-
"tue is to find its reward. She thinks no one
"so unhappy as herself; but if she knew all

"that

" that you have gone through, she would surely
" be fenfible, that if you are happier than she, it
" is only becaufe your principles are better."

" INDEED, my dear madam," said she, " that
" is the only advantage I have over you ; but
" that, indeed, outweighs every thing elfe.
" It is now but ten days fince I followed to the
" grave my only fon, the furvivor of eight
" children, who were all equally the objects of
" my fondeft love.   My heart is no lefs tender
" than your own, nor my affections lefs warm.
" For a whole year before the death of my laft
" darling, I· watched the fatal progrefs of his
" difeafe, and faw him fuffer the moft amazing
" pains.   Nor was poverty, that dreaded evil
" to which you could not fubmit, wanting to
" my trials.   Though my hufband is by his
" profeffion a gentleman, his income is fo fmall,
" that I and my children have often wanted
" neceffaries : and though I had always a
" weakly conftitution, I have helped to fupport
" my family by the labour of my own hands.
" At this time I am confuming, by daily tor-
" tures, with a cancer which muft fhortly be
" my death.   My pains, perhaps, might be mi-
" tigated by proper affiftance, though nothing
" could preferve my life ; but I have not the
" means to obtain that affiftance."——O hold,
interrupted I, my foul is fhocked at the enumeration

ration of such intolerable sufferings.   How is it
that you support them?  Why do I not see you,
in despair like mine, renounce your existence,
and put yourself out of the reach of torment?
But above all, tell me how it is possible for you
to preserve, amidst such complicated misery, that
appearance of cheerfulness and serene complacency which shines so remarkably in your countenance, and animates every look and motion?

" THAT cheerfulness and complacency," an-
swered the good woman, " I feel in my heart.
" My mind is not only serene, but often expe-
" riences the highest emotions of joy and exul-
" tation, that the brightest hopes can give."
And whence, said I, do you derive this asto-
nishing art of extracting joy from misery, and of
smiling amidst all the terrors of pain, sorrow,
poverty, and death?  She was silent a moment;
then stepping to her closet, reached a BIBLE,
which she put into my hands.  " See there,"
said she, " the volume in which I learn this art.
" Here I am taught, that everlasting glory is in
" store for all who will accept it upon the
" terms which INFINITE PERFECTION has pre-
" scribed; here I am promised consolation, af-
" sistance and support from the LORD OF LIFE;
" and here I am assured that my transient
" afflictions are only meant to fit me for eternal
" and unspeakable happiness.  This happiness
" is

" is at hand.   The fhort remainder of my life
" feems but a point, beyond which opens the
" glorious profpect of immortality.   Thus en-
" couraged, how fhould I be dejected ? Thus
" fupported, how fhould I fink ? With fuch
" profpects, fuch affured hopes, how can I be
" otherwife than happy ?"

WHILE fhe fpoke, her eyes fparkled, and her
whole face feemed animated with joy.   I was
ftruck with her manner, as well as her words.
Every fyllable fhe uttered feemed to fink into my
foul, fo that I never can forget it.   I refolved to
examine a religion, which was capable of producing fuch effects as I could not attribute either
to chance or error.   The good couple preffed
me with fo much unaffected kindnefs, to make
their little parfonage my afylum till I could better
difpofe of myfelf, that I accepted their offer.
Here, with the affiftance of the clergyman, who
is a plain, fenfible, and truly pious man, I have
ftudied the HOLY SCRIPTURES, and the evidences
of their authority.   But after reading them with
candour and attention, I found all the extrinfic
arguments of their truth fuperfluous.   The excel-
lency of their precepts, the confiftency of their
doctrines, and the glorious motives and encou-
ragements to virtue which they propofe, together
with the ftriking example I had before my eyes

of

of their falutary effects, left me no doubt of their divine authority.

DURING the time of my abode here, I have been witnefs to the more than heroic, the joyful, the triumphant death of the dear good woman. With as much foftnefs and tendernefs as ever I faw in a female character, fhe fhewed more dauntlefs intrepidity than the fterneft philofopher or the proudeft hero. No torment could fhake the conftancy of her foul, or length of pain wear out the ftrength of her patience. Death was to her an object not of horror but of hope. When I heard her pour forth her laft breath in thankfgiving, and faw the fmile of extafy remain on her pale face when life was fled, I could not help crying out in the beautiful language I had lately learned from the SACRED WRITINGS, "O Death! where is thy fting? O Grave! "where is thy victory?"

I AM now preparing to leave my excellent benefactor, and get my bread in a fervice, to which he has recommended me, in a neighbouring family. A ftate of fervitude, to which once I could not refolve to yield, appears no longer dreadful to me; that pride, which would have made it galling, CHRISTIANITY has fubdued, though philofophy attempted it in vain. As a penitent, I fhould gratefully fubmit to mortification; but as a CHRISTIAN, I find myfelf fuperior
rior

rior to every mortification, except the fenfe of guilt. This has humbled me to the duft: but the full affurances that are given me by the SA-VIOUR OF THE WORLD, of the DIVINE pardon and favour upon fincere repentance, have calmed my troubled fpirit, and filled my mind with peace and joy, which the world can neither give nor take away. Thus, without any change for the better in my outward circumftances, I find my-felf changed from a diftracted, poor, defpairing wretch, to a contented, happy, grateful being; thankful for, and pleafed with my prefent ftate of exiftence, yet exulting in the hope of quitting it for endlefs glory and happinefs.

O! SIR, tell the unthinking mortals, who will not take the pains of inquiring into thofe truths which moft concern them, and who are led by fafhion, and the pride of human reafon, into a contempt for the SACRED ORACLES of GOD; tell them thefe amazing effects of the power of CHRISTIANITY: tell them this truth which experience has taught me, that, " Though " VICE is conftantly attended by mifery, VIRTUE " itfelf cannot confer happinefs in this world, ex- " cept it is animated with the hopes of eternal " blifs in the world to come.

Y    I am, &c.

FIDELIA."

NUMB. 80.   SATURDAY, *August* 11, 1753.

*Non desunt crassi quidam, qui studiosos ab hujus-*
*modi libris deterreant, ceu poeticis, ut vocant, &*
*ad morum integritatem officientibus.   Ego vero dig-*
*nos censeo quos &. omnibus in ludis prælegant*
*adolescentiæ literatores, & sibi legant relegantque*
*senes.*                              ERASMUS.

There are not wanting persons so dull and in-
sensible, as to deter students from reading books
of this kind, which, they say, are poetical, and
pernicious to the purity of morals : but I am of
opinion, that they are not only worthy to be read
by the instructors of youth in their schools, but
that the old and experienced should again and
again peruse them.

GREATNESS, novelty, and beauty, are
usually and justly reckoned the three principal sources of the pleasures that strike the imagination.   If the ILIAD be allowed to abound
in objects that may be referred to the first species,
yet the ODYSSEY may boast a greater number of
images that are beautiful and uncommon.   The
vast variety of scenes perpetually shifting before
us, the train of unexpected events, and the
many sudden turns of fortune in this diversified
poem, must more deeply engage the reader, and
                                              keep

keep his attention more alive and active, than the
martial uniformity of the ILIAD.  The continual glare of a single colour that unchangeably
predominates throughout a whole piece, is apt to
dazzle and difguft the eye of the beholder.  I will
not, indeed, prefume to fay with VOLTAIRE,
that among the greateft admirers of antiquity,
there is fcarce one to be found, who could ever
read the ILIAD with that eagernefs and rapture,
which a woman feels when fhe perufes the novel
of ZAYDE; but will, however, venture to affirm, that the SPECIOSA MIRACULA of the
ODYSSEY are better calculated to excite our
curiofity and wonder, and to allure us forward
with unextinguifhed impatience to the cataftro-
phe, than the perpetual tumult and terror that
reign through the ILIAD.

THE boundlefs exuberance of his imagination,
his unwearied fpirit and fire, ἀκάματον πῦρ, has
enabled HOMER to diverfify the defcriptions of
his battles with many circumftances of great
variety: fometimes, by fpecifying the different
characters, ages, profeffions, or nations, of his
dying heroes; fometimes by defcribing different
kinds of wounds and deaths; and fometimes by
tender and pathetic ftrokes, which remind the
reader of the aged parent who is fondly expecting the return of his fon juft murdered, of the
defolate condition of the widows who will now
be

he enflaved, and of the children that will be
dafhed againft the ftones.    But notwithftanding
this delicate art and addrefs in the poet, the
fubject remains the fame; and from this fame-
nefs, it will, I fear, grow tedious and infipid to
impartial readers; thefe fmall modifications and
adjuncts are not fufficiently efficacious to give
the grace of novelty to repetition, and to make
tautology delightful: the battles, are, indeed,
nobly and varioufly painted, yet ftill they are
only battles. But when we accompany ULYSSES
through the manifold perils he underwent by fea
and land, and vifit with him the ftrange nations
to which the anger of Neptune has driven him,
all whofe manners and cuftoms are defcribed in
the moft lively and picturefque terms; when
we furvey the wondrous monfters he encoun-
tered and efcaped,

*Antiphaten, Scyllamque, & eum Cyclope Charibdin;*

Antiphates his hideous feaft devour,
Charybdis bark and Polyphemus roar; FRANCIS.

when we fee him refufe the charms of Calypfo,
and the cup of Circe; when we defcend with
him into hell, and hear him converfe with all
the glorious heroes that affifted at the Trojan
war; when, after ftruggling with ten thoufand
difficulties unforefeen and almoft unfurmount-
able, he is at laft reftored to the peaceable pof-

feffion of his kingdom and his queen; when fuch
objects as thefe are difplayed, fo new and fo interefting; when all the defcriptions, incidents,
fcenes, and perfons, differ fo widely from each
other; then it is that poetry becomes " a per-
" petual feaft of nectared fweets," and a feaft
of fuch an exalted nature, as to produce neither
fatiety or difguft.

BUT befides its variety, the ODYSSEY is the
moft amufing and entertaining of all other poems,
on account of the pictures it preferves to us of
ancient manners, cuftoms, laws, and politics,
and of the domeftic life of the heroic ages. The
more any nation becomes polifhed, the more the
genuine feelings of nature are difguifed, and their
manners are confequently lefs adapted to bear a
faithful defcription. Good-breeding is founded
on the fuppreffion of fuch fentiments, as may probably provoke or offend thofe
with whom we converfe. The little forms and
ceremonies which have been introduced into civil
life by the moderns, are not fuited to the dignity
and fimplicity of the EPIC MUSE. The corona-
tion feaft of an European monarch would not
fhine half fo much in poetry, as the fimple fup-
per prepared for ULYSSES at the Phæacian
court; the gardens of ALCINOUS are much fitter
for defcription than thofe of Verfailles; and
NAUSICAA, defcending to the river to wafh her
garments,

garments, and dancing afterwards upon the
banks with her fellow-virgins, like Diana amidst
her nymphs,

'Ρεῖα δ᾽ ἀριγνώτω πέλεται, καλαὶ δέ τε πᾶσαι,

Tho' all are fair, she shines above the rest,

is a far more graceful figure, than the most glittering lady in the drawing-room, with a complexion plaistered to repair the vigils of cards,
and a shape violated by a stiff brocade and an im-
measurable hoop.   The compliment also which
ULYSSES pays to his innocent unadorned beauty,
especially when he compares her to a young
palm-tree of Delos, contains more gallantry and
elegance, than the most applauded sonnet of the
politest French marquis that ever rhymed.   However indelicate I may be esteemed, I freely confess I had rather sit in the grotto of CALYPSO,
than in the most pompous saloon of LOUIS XV.
The tea and the card-tables can be introduced
with propriety and success only in the mock-
heroic, as they have been very happily in the
Rape of the Lock: but the present modes of
life must be forgotten when we attempt any
thing in the serious or sublime poetry; for hero-
ism disdains the luxurious refinements, the false
delicacy and state of modern ages.   The prime-
val, I was about to say, patriarchal simplicity of

manners difplayed in the ODYSSEY, is a perpetual fource of true poetry, is inexpreffibly pleafing to all who are uncorrupted by the bufinefs
and the vanities of life, and may therefore prove
equally inftructive and captivating to younger
readers.

IT feems to be a tenet univerfally received
among common critics, as certain and indifput-
able, that images and characters of peaceful and
domeftic life are not fo difficult to be drawn, as
pictures of war and fury. I own myfelf of a
quite contrary opinion; and think the defcription of Andromache parting with Hector in the
ILIAD, and the tender circumftance of the child
Aftyanax ftarting back from his father's helmet,
and clinging to the bofom of his nurfe, are as
great efforts of the imagination of HOMER, as
the dreadful picture of Achilles fighting with the
rivers, or dragging the carcafs of Hector at his
chariot-wheels : the behaviour of HECUBA,
when fhe points to the breaft that had fuckled
her dear HECTOR, is as finely conceived as the
moft gallant exploits of DIOMEDE and AJAX :
the NATURAL is as ftrong an evidence of true
genius, as the SUBLIME. It is in fuch images
the ODYSSEY abounds : the fuperior utility of
which, as they more nearly concern and more
ftrongly affect us, need not be pointed out. Let
LONGINUS admire the majefty of Neptune whirling

ing his chariot over the deep, surrounded by sea
monsters that gambolled before their king; the
description of the dog Argus, creeping to the feet
of his master, whom he alone knew in his disguise, and expiring with joy for his return, is so
inexpressibly pathetic, that it equals, if not exceeds
any of the magnificent and bolder images which
that excellent critic hath produced in his treatise
on the sublime.  He justly commends the prayer
of Ajax, who, when he was surrounded with a
thick darkness that prevented the display of his
prowess, begs of Jupiter only to remove the
clouds that involved him;  " and then," says he,
" destroy me if thou wilt in the day-light;"
ἐν δὲ Φάει καὶ ὄλεσσον.   But surely the reflections
which ULYSSES makes to Amphinomus, the most
virtuous of the suitors, concerning the misery
and vanity of man, will be found to deserve equal
commendations, if we consider their propriety,
solemnity, and truth.   Our hero, in the disguise
of a beggar, had just been spurned at and ridiculed by the rest of the riotous lovers, but is
kindly relieved by Amphinomus, whose behaviour is finely contrasted to the brutality of his
brethren.   Upon which ULYSSES says, " Hear
" me, O Amphinomus! and ponder the words
" I shall speak unto thee.  Of all creatures that
" breathe or creep upon the earth, the most
" weak and impotent is man.  For he never

" thinks

" thinks that evils fhall befal him at another
" feafon, while the Gods beftow on him ftrength
" and happinefs. But when the immortal Gods
" afflict him with adverfity, he bears it with un-
" willingnefs and repining. Such is the mind
" of the inhabitants of earth, that it changes as
" Jupiter fends happinefs or mifery. I once
" numbered myfelf among the happy, and elated
" with profperity and pride, and relying on my
" family and friends, committed many acts of
" injuftice. But let no man be proud or unjuft,
" but receive whatever gifts the Gods beftow on
" him with humility and filence." I chofe to
tranflate this fententious paffage as literally as
poffible, to preferve the air of its venerable fimplicity and ftriking folemnity. If we recollect
the fpeaker, and the occafion of the fpeech, we
cannot fail of being deeply affected. Can we,
therefore, forbear giving our affent to the truth
of the title which ALCIDAMAS, according to
ARISTOTLE in his rhetoric, beftows on the
ODYSSEY; who calls it " a beautiful mirror of
" human life," καλὸν ἀνθρωπίνε βίε κάτοπ]ρον.

HOMER, in the ILIAD, refembles the river
Nile, when it defcends in a cataract that deafens
and aftonifhes the neighbouring inhabitants. In
the ODYSSEY, he is ftill like the fame Nile, when
its genial inundations gently diffufe fertility and
fatnefs over the peaceful plains of Egypt.

Z

Numb. 81.  Tuesday, *August* 14, 1753.

*Nil desperandum.*  Hor.
Avaunt despair.

I HAVE sometimes heard it disputed in conversation, whether it be more laudable or
desirable, that a man should think too highly or
too meanly of himself: it is on all hands agreed
to be best, that he should think rightly: but
since a fallible being will always make some de-
viations from exact rectitude, it is not wholly
useless to enquire towards which side it is safer
to decline.

THE prejudices of mankind seem to favour
him who errs by under-rating his own powers;
he is considered as a modest and harmless member of society, not likely to break the peace by
competition, to endeavour after such splendor of
reputation as may dim the lustre of others, or to
interrupt any in the enjoyment of themselves;
he is no man's rival, and, therefore, may be
every man's friend.

THE opinion which a man entertains of himself ought to be distinguished, in order to an ac-
curate discussion of this question, as it relates to
persons or to things.  To think highly of ourselves in comparison with others, to assume by
our own authority that precedence which none

is willing to grant, muſt be always invidious and offenſive ; but to rate our powers high in proportion to things, and imagine ourſelves equal to great undertakings, while we leave others in poſſeſſion of the ſame abilities, cannot with equal juſtice provoke cenſure.

It muſt be confeſſed, that ſelf-love may diſpoſe us to decide too haſtily in our own favour : but who is hurt by the miſtake ? If we are incited by this vain opinion to attempt more than we can perform, ours is the labour, and ours is the diſgrace.

But he that dares to think well of himſelf, will not always prove to be miſtaken ; and the good effects of his confidence will then appear in great attempts and great performances : if he ſhould not fully compleat his deſign, he will at leaſt advance it ſo far as to leave an eaſier taſk for him that ſucceeds him ; and even though he ſhould wholly fail, he will fail with honour.

But from the oppoſite error, from torpid deſpondency can come no advantage ; it is the froſt of the ſoul, which binds up all its powers, and congeals life in perpetual ſterility. He that has no hopes of ſucceſs, will make no attempts ; and where nothing is attempted, nothing can be done.

Every man ſhould, therefore, endeavour to maintain in himſelf a favourable opinion of the

powers

powers of the human mind; which are perhaps, in every man, greater than they appear, and might, by diligent cultivation, be exalted to a degree beyond what their poffeffor prefumes to believe. There is fcarce any man but has found himfelf able, at the inftigation of neceffity, to do what in a ftate of leifure and deliberation he would have concluded impoffible; and fome of our fpecies have fignalized themfelves by fuch atchievements, as prove that there are few things above human hope.

It has been the policy of all nations to pre-ferve, by fome public monuments, the memory of thofe who have ferved their country by great exploits; there is the fame reafon for continuing or reviving the names of thofe, whofe extenfive abilities have dignified humanity. An honeft emulation may be alike excited; and the philo-fopher's curiofity may be inflamed by a catalogue of the works of Boyle or Bacon, as Themiftocles was kept awake by the trophies of Miltiades.

Among the favourites of nature that have from time to time appeared in the world, en-riched with various endowments and contra-rieties of excellence, none feems to have been more exalted above the common rate of hu-manity, than the man known about two centu-ries ago by the appellation of the ADMIRABLE CRICHTON; of whofe hiftory, whatever we may -

fupprefs

,fupprefs as furpaffing credibility, yet we fhall,
upon inconteftible authority, relate enough to
rank him among prodigies.

"VIRTUE," fays Virgi', "is better accepted
"when it comes in a pleafing form:" the perfon
of CRICHTON was eminently beautiful; but his
beauty was confiftent with fuch activity and
ftrength, that in fencing he would fpring at one
bound the length of twenty feet upon his antagonift; and he ufed the fword in either hand with
fuch force and dexterity, that fcarce any one had
courage to engage him.

HAVING ftudied at St. Andrew's in Scotland
he went to Paris in his twenty-firft year, and
affixed on the gate of the college of Navarre a
kind of challenge to the learned of that univerfity
to difpute with him on a certain day: offering to
his opponents, whoever they fhould be, the
choice of ten languages, and of all the faculties
and fciences. On the day appointed three thoufand auditors affembled, when four doctors of
the church and fifty mafters appeared againft
him; and one of his antagonifts confeffes, that
the doctors were defeated; that he gave proofs
of knowledge above the reach of man; and that
a hundred years paffed without food or fleep,
would not be fufficient for the attainment of his
learning. After a difputation of nine hours he
was prefented by the prefident and profeffors
                                                        with

with a diamond and a purſe of gold, and diſ-
miſſed with repeated acclamations.

FROM Paris he went away to Rome, where
he made the ſame challenge, and had in the
preſence of the pope and cardinals the ſame
ſucceſs.   Afterwards he contracted at Venice an
acquaintance with Aldus Manutius, by whom he
was introduced to the learned of that city : then
viſited Padua, where he engaged in another
public diſputation, .beginning his performance ›
with an extemporal poem in praiſe of the city
and the aſſembly then preſent, and concluding
with an oration equally unpremeditated in commendation of ignorance.

HE afterwards publiſhed another challenge, in
which he declared himſelf ready to detect the
errors of Ariſtotle and all his commentators,
either in the common forms of logic, or in any
which his antagoniſts ſhould propoſe of a hundred different kinds of verſe.

THESE acquiſitions of learning, however ſtu-
pendous, were not gained at the expence of any
pleaſure which youth generally indulges, or by
the omiſſion of any accompliſhment in which it
becomes a gentleman to excel : he practiſed in
great perfection the arts of drawing and painting,
he was an eminent performer in both vocal and
inſtrumental muſic, he danced with uncommon
gracefulneſs, and on the day after his diſputation

F 3                              at

at Paris exhibited his skill in horsemanship before
the court of France, where, at a public match of
tilting, he bore away the ring upon his lance
fifteen times together.

HE excelled likewise in domestic games of
less dignity and reputation ; and in the interval
between his challenge and disputation at Paris,
he spent so much of his time at cards, dice, and
tennis, that a lampoon was fixed upon the gate
of the Sorbonne, directing those that would see
this monster of erudition, to look for him at the
tavern.

So extensive was his acquaintance with life
and manners, that in an Italian comedy, com-
posed by himself, and exhibited before the court
of Mantua, he is said to have personated fifteen
different characters ; in all which he might suc-
ceed without great difficulty, since he had such
power of retention, that once hearing an oration
of an hour, he would repeat it exactly, and in
the recital follow the speaker through all his variety of tone and gesticulation.

NOR was his skill in arms less than in learning,
or his courage inferior to his skill : there was a
prize-fighter at Mantua, who travelling about
the world, according to the barbarous custom of
that age, as a general challenger, had defeated
the most celebrated masters in many parts of
Europe ; and in Mantua, where he then resided,

had

had killed three that appeared against him. The
duke repented that he had granted him his protection; when CRICHTON, looking on his fanguinary fuccefs with indignation, offered to ftake
fifteen hundred piftoles, and mount the ftage
againft him. The duke, with fome reluctance,
confented, and on the day fixed the combatants
appeared: their weapon feems to have been fingle
rapier, which was then newly introduced in
Italy. The prize-fighter advanced with great
violence and fiercenefs, and CRICHTON contented himfelf calmly to ward his paffes, and
fuffered him to exhauft his vigour by his own
fury. CRICHTON then became the affailant;
and preffed upon him with fuch force and agility,
that he thruft him thrice through the body, and
-faw him expire: he then divided the prize he
had won among the widows whofe hufbands had
been killed.

THE death of this wonderful man I fhould be
willing to conceal, did I not know that every
reader will inquire curioufly after that fatal hour,
which is common to all human beings, however diftinguifhed from each other by nature or
by fortune.

. THE duke of Mantua having received fo
many proofs of his various merit, made him tutor
to his fon Vincentio di Gonzaga, a prince of
loofe manners and turbulent difpofition. On this

occafion it was, that he compofed the comedy
in which he exhibited fo many different characters with exact propriety.　But his honour was
of fhort continuance; for as he was one night
in the time of Carnival rambling about the
ftreets, with his guitar in his hand, he was
attacked by fix men mafked.　Neither his courage
nor fkill in this exigence deferted him; he oppofed them with fuch activity and fpirit, that he
foon difperfed them, and difarmed their leader,
who throwing off his mafk, difcovered himfelf to
be the prince his pupil.　CRICHTON falling on
his knees, took his own fword by the point, and
prefented it to the prince; who immediately
feized it, and inftigated, as fome fay, by jealoufy,
according to others, only by drunken fury and
brutal refentment, thruft him through the heart.

THUS was the ADMIRABLE CRICHTON
brought into that ftate, in which he could excel
the meaneft of mankind only by a few empty honours paid to his memory: the court of Mantua
teftified their efteem by a public mourning, the
contemporary wits were profufe of their enco-
miums, and the palaces of Italy were adorned
with pictures, reprefenting him on horfeback
with a lance in one hand and a book in the other.

NUMB. 82. SATURDAY, *August* 18, 1753.

*Nunc scio quid fit* AMOR. VIRG.

Now know I what is love.

THOUGH the danger of difappointment is always in proportion to the height of expectation, yet I this day claim the attention of the ladies, and profefs to teach an art by which all may obtain what has hitherto been deemed the prerogative of a few; an art by which their predominant paffion may be gratified, and their conquefts not only extended but fecured; "The " art of being PRETTY."

BUT though my fubject may intereft the ladies, it may, perhaps, offend thofe profound moralifts, who have long fince determined, that BEAUTY ought rather to be defpifed than defired; that, like ftrength, it is a mere natural excellence, the effect of caufes wholly out of our power, and not intended either as the pledge of happinefs or the diftinction of merit.

. To thefe gentlemen I fhall remark, that beauty is among thofe qualities, which no effort of human wit could ever bring into contempt: it is, therefore, to be wifhed at leaft, that beauty was in fome degree dependent upon SENTIMENT and

F 5 MANNERS,

MANNERS, that so high a privilege might not be possessed by the unworthy, and that human reason might no longer suffer the mortification of those who are compelled to adore an idol, which differs from a stone or a log only by the skill of the artificer: and if they cannot themselves behold beauty with indifference, they must surely approve an attempt to shew that it merits their regard.

I SHALL, however, principally consider that species of beauty which is expressed in the countenance; for this alone is peculiar to human beings, and is not less complicated than their nature. In the countenance there are but two requisites to perfect BEAUTY, which are wholly produced by external causes, colour and proportion: and it will appear, that even in common estimation these are not the chief, but that though there may be beauty without them, yet there cannot be beauty without something more.

THE finest features, ranged in the most exact symmetry, and heightened by the most blooming complexion, must be animated before they can strike: and when they are animated, will generally excite the same passions which they express. If they are fixed in the dead calm of insensibility, they will be examined without emotion; and if they do not express kindness, they will be beheld without love. Looks of contempt, disdain, or

malevolence,

malevolence, will be reflected, as from a mirror, by every countenance on which they are turned ; and if a wanton aspect excites desire, it is but like that of a savage for his prey, which cannot be gratified without the destruction of its object.

AMONG particular graces the dimple has always been allowed the pre-eminence, and the reason is evident ; dimples are produced by a smile, and a smile is an expression of complacency : so the contraction of the brows into a frown, as it is an indication of a contrary temper, has always been deemed a capital defect.

THE lover is generally at a loss to define the beauty, by which his passion was suddenly and irresistibly determined to a particular object ; but this could never happen, if it depended upon any known rule of proportion, upon the shape or disposition of the features, or the colour of the skin : he tells you, that it is something which he cannot fully express, something not fixed in any part, but diffused over the whole ; he calls it a sweetness, a softness, a placid sensibility, or gives it some other appellation which connects beauty with SENTIMENT, and expresses a charm which is not peculiar to any set of features, but is perhaps possible to all.

THIS beauty, however, does not always consist in smiles, but varies as expressions of meekness and kindness vary with their objects ; it is

F 6        extremely

extremely forcible in the filent complaint of patient fufferance, the tender folicitude of friendfhip, and the glow of filial obedience; and in
tears whether of joy, of pity, or of grief, it is
almoft irrefiftible.

THIS is the charm which captivates without
the aid of nature, and without which her utmoft bounty is ineffectual. But it cannot be
affumed as a mafk to conceal infenfibility or
malevolence; it muft be the genuine effect of
correfponding fentiments, or it will imprefs
upon the countenance a new and more difguft-
ing deformity, AFFECTATION; it will produce
the grin, the fimper, the ftare, the languifh, the
pout, and innumerable other grimaces, that render folly ridiculous, and change pity to contempt. By fome, indeed, this fpecies of hypocrify has been practifed with fuch fkill as to
deceive fuperficial obfervers, though it can deceive even thefe but for a moment. Looks
which do not correfpond with the heart, cannot
be affumed without labour, nor continued without pain; the motive to relinquifh them muft,
therefore, foon preponderate, and the afpect and
apparel of the vifit will be laid by together; the
fmiles and the languifhments of art will vanifh,
and the fiercenefs of rage, or the gloom of difcontent, will either obfcure or deftroy all the
elegance of fymmetry and complexion.

THE

THE artificial afpect is, indeed, as wretched a fubftitute for the expreffion of fentiment, as the fmear of paint for the blufhes of health : it is not only equally tranfient, and equally liable to detection ; but as paint leaves the countenance yet more withered and ghaftly, the paffions burft out with more violence after reftraint, the features become more diftorted, and excite more determined averfion.

BEAUTY, therefore, depends principally upon the mind, and confequently may be influenced by education. It has been remarked, that the predominant paffion may generally be difcovered in the countenance ; becaufe the mufcles by which it is expreffed, being almoft perpetually contracted, lofe their tone, and never totally relax ; fo that the expreffion remains when the paffion is fufpended : thus an angry, a difdainful, a fubtle, and a fufpicious temper, is difplayed in characters that are almoft univerfally underftood. It is equally true of the pleafing and the fofter paffions, that they leave their fignatures upon the countenance when they ceafe to act : the prevalence of thefe paffions, therefore, produces a mechanical effect upon the afpect, and gives a turn and caft to the features which make a more favourable and forcible impreffion upon the mind of others, than any charm produced by mere external caufes.

NEITHER

NEITHER does the beauty which depends upon temper and sentiment, equally endanger the possessor; " It is," to use an eastern metaphor, " like the towers of a city, not only an orna- " ment, but a defence:" if it excites desire, it at once controuls and refines it; it represses with awe, it softens with delicacy, and it wins to imitation. The love of reason and of virtue is mingled with the love of beauty; because this beauty is little more than the emanation of intellectual excellence, which is not an object of corporeal appetite. As it excites a purer passion, it also more forcibly engages to fidelity: every man finds himself more powerfully re- strained from giving pain to goodness than to beauty; and every look of a countenance in which they are blended, in which beauty is the expression of goodness, is a silent reproach of the first irregular wish; and the purpose imme- diately appears to be disingenuous and cruel, by which the tender hope of ineffable affection would be disappointed, the placid confidence of unsuspecting simplicity abused, and the peace even of virtue endangered, by the most sordid infidelity, and the breach of the strongest obli- gations.

BUT the hope of the hypocrite must perish. When the factitious beauty has laid by her smiles; when the lustre of her eyes and the bloom of

her

her cheeks have loft their influence with their novelty; what remains but a tyrant divefted of power, who will never be feen without a mixture of indignation and difdain? The only defire which this object could gratify, will be tranf- ferred to another, not only without reluctance, but with triumph. As refentment will fucceed to difappointment, a defire to mortify will fuc- ceed to a defire to pleafe; and the hufband may be urged to folicit a miftrefs, merely by a re- membrance of the beauty of his wife, which lafted only till fhe was known.

LET it, therefore, be remembered, that none can be difciples of the GRACES, but in the fchool of VIRTUE; and that thofe who wifh to be LOVELY, muft learn early to be GOOD.

NUMB. 83.   TUESDAY, *August* 21, 1753.

*Illic enim debet toto animo a poetâ in diffolutionem
nodi, agi; eaque præcipua fabulæ pars eft quæ re-
quirit plurimum diligentiæ.*    CICERO.

The poet ought to exert his whole ftrength
and fpirit in the folution of his plot; which is
the principal part of the fable, and requires the
utmoft diligence and care.

OF the three only perfect EPOPEES, which,
in the compafs of fo many ages, human
wit has been able to produce, the conduct and
conftitution of the ODYSSEY feem to be the
moft artificial and judicious.

ARISTOTLE obferves, that there are two kinds
of fables, the fimple and the complex. A fable
in tragic or epic poetry, is denominated fimple,
when the events it contains follow each other
in a continued and unbroken tenour, without a
RECOGNITION or difcovery, and without a PE-
RIPETIE or unexpected change of fortune. A
fable is called complex, when it contains both a
difcovery and a peripetie. And this great critic,
whofe knowledge of human nature was con-
fummate, determines, that fables of the latter
fpecies far excel thofe of the former, becaufe
they

they more deeply intereſt and more irreſiſtibly move the reader, by adding ſurprize and aſtoniſhment to every other paſſion which they excite.

THE philoſopher, agreeably to this obſervation, prefers the ŒDIPUS of SOPHOCLES, and the IPHIGENIA in Tauris and ALCESTES of EURIPIDES, to the AJAX, PHILOCTETES, and MEDEA of the ſame writers, and to the PROMETHEUS of ESCHYLUS : becauſe theſe laſt are all uncomplicated fables ; that is, the evils and misfortunes that befal the perſonages repreſented in theſe dramas, are unchangeably continued from the beginning to the end of each piece. For the ſame reaſons, the ATHALIAH of RACINE, and the MEROPE's of MAFFEI and VOLTAIRE, are beyond compariſon the moſt affecting ſtories that have been handled by any modern tragic writer: the diſcoveries, that JOAS is the king of Iſrael, and that EGISTUS is the ſon of MEROPE, who had juſt ordered him to be murdered, are ſo unexpected, but yet ſo probable, that they may juſtly be eſteemed very great efforts of judgment and genius, and contribute to place theſe two poems at the head of dramatic compoſitions.

THE fable of the ODYSSEY being complex, and containing a diſcovery and a change in the fortune of its hero, is upon this ſingle conſideration, excluſive of its other beauties, if we follow

the

the principles of ARISTOTLE, much superior to the fables of the ILIAD and the ÆNEID, which are both simple and unadorned with a peripetie or recognition.    The naked story of this poem, stript of all its ornaments, and of the very names of the characters, is exhibited by ARISTOTLE in the following paſſage, which is almoſt literally tranſlated.

" A MAN is for ſeveral years abſent from his " home ; Neptune continually watches and per- " ſecutes him ; his retinue being deſtroyed, he " remains alone : but while his eſtate is waſting " by the ſuitors of his wife, and his ſon's life is " plotted againſt, he himſelf ſuddenly arrives " after many ſtorms at ſea, diſcovers himſelf to " ſome of his friends, falls on the ſuitors, eſta- " bliſhes himſelf in ſafety, and deſtroys his ene- " mies.    This is what is eſſential to the fable ; " the epiſodes make up the reſt."

FROM theſe obſervations on the nature of the fable of the ODYSSEY in general, we may pro- ceed to conſider it more minutely.    The two chief parts of every epic fable are its INTRIGUE or PLOT, and its SOLUTION or UNRAVELLING. The intrigue is formed by a complication of dif- ferent intereſts, which keep the mind of the reader in a pleaſing ſuſpence, and fill him with anxious wiſhes to ſee the obſtacles that oppoſe the deſigns of the hero happily removed.    The ſolution folution confifts in removing thefe difficulties,. in fatisfying the curiofity of the reader by the completion of the intended action, and in leaving his mind in perfect repofe, without expectation of any farther event. Both of thefe fhould arife naturally and eafily out of the very effence and fubject of the poem itfelf, fhould not be deduced from circumftances foreign and extrinfical, fhould be at the fame time probable yet wonderful.

THE anger of Neptune, who refented the punifhment which ULYSSES had inflicted on his fon Polypheme, induces him to prevent the return of the hero to Ithaca, by driving him from country to country by violent tempefts; and from this indignation of Neptune is formed the intrigue of the ODYSSEY in the firft part of the poem; that is, in plain profe, " what more " natural and ufual obftacle do they encounter " who take long voyages, than the violence of " winds and ftorms ?" The plot of the fecond part of the poem is founded on circumftances. equally probable and natural; on the unavoidable effects of the long abfence of a mafter, whofe return was defpaired of, the infolence of his. fervants, the dangers to which his wife and his. fon were expofed, the ruin of his eftate, and the diforder of his kingdom..

THE

THE addreſs and art of HOMER in the gradual
ſolution of this plot, by the moſt probable and
eaſy expedients, are equally worthy our admiration and applauſe.    ULYSSES is driven by a
tempeſt to the iſland of the Phæacians, where he
is generouſly and hoſpitably received.    During a
banquet which Alcinous the king has prepared
for him, the poet moſt artfully contrives that the
bard Demodocus ſhould ſing the deſtruction of
Troy.    At the recital of his paſt labours, and
at hearing the names of his old companions, from
whom he was now ſeparated, our hero could no
longer contain himſelf, but burſt into tears and
weeps bitterly.    The curioſity of Alcinous being
excited by this unaccountable ſorrow, he intreats
ULYSSES 'to diſcover who he is, and what he
has ſuffered ;  which requeſt furniſhes a moſt proper and probable occaſion to the hero to relate
a long ſeries of adventures in the four following
books, an occaſion much more natural than that
which induces Æneas to communicate his hiſtory to Dido.    By this judicious conduct, Ho-
MER taught his ſucceſſors the artful manner of
entering abruptly into the midſt of the action ;
and of making the reader acquainted with the
previous circumſtances by a narrative from the
hero.    The Phæacians, a people fond of ſtrange
and amuſing tales, reſolved to fit out a ſhip for
the diſtreſſed hero, as a reward for the entertainment

tainment he has given them. When he arrives in Ithaca, his abfence, his age, and his travels, render him totally unknown to all but his faithful dog Argus : he then puts on a difguife, that he may be the better enabled to furprize and to punifh the riotous fuitors, and to re-eftablifh the tranquillity of his kingdom. The reader thinks that ULYSSES is frequently on the point of being difcovered, particularly when he engages in the fhooting-match with the fuitors, and when he enters into converfation with Penelope in the nineteenth book, and perfonates a fictitious character ; but he is ftill judicioufly difappointed, and the fufpence is kept up as long as poffible. And at laft, when his nurfe EURICLEA difcovers him by the fcar in his thigh, it is a circumftance fo fimple and fo natural, that notwithftanding ARISTOTLE places thefe recognitions, by SIGNS and TOKENS, below thofe that are effected by REASONING, as in the Oedipus and Iphigenia ; yet ought it ever to be remembered, that HOMER was the original from whom this ftriking method of unravelling a fable, by a difcovery and a peripetie, was manifeftly borrowed. The doubts and fears of Penelope left ULYSSES was not in reality her hufband, and the tendernefs and endearments that enfue upon her conviction that he is, render the furprize and fatisfaction of the reader compleat.

UPON

UPON the whole, the ODYSSEY is a poem that exhibits the fineſt leſſons of morality, the moſt entertaining variety of ſcenes and events, the moſt lively and natural pictures of civil and domeſtic life, the trueſt repreſentation of the manners and cuſtoms of antiquity, and the juſteſt pattern of a legitimate EPOPEE: and is, therefore, peculiarly uſeful to thoſe, who are animated by the noble ambition of adorning humanity by living or by writing well.

Z

*****************************

NUMB. 84.    SATURDAY, *Auguſt* 25, 1753.

————————*Tolle periculum,*
*Jam vaga proſiliå frænis natura remotis.*    HOR.

But take the danger and the ſhame away,
And vagrant nature bounds upon her prey.
                                        FRANCIS.

To the ADVENTURER.

SIR,

IT has been obſerved, I think, by Sir WIL-LIAM TEMPLE, and after him by almoſt every other writer, that England affords a greater variety of characters than the reſt of the world. This

This is afcribed to the liberty prevailing amongft us, which gives every man the privilege of being wife or foolifh his own way, and preferves him from the neceffity of hypocrify or the fervility of imitation.

THAT the pofition itfelf is true, I am not completely fatisfied. To be nearly acquainted with the people of different countries can happen to very few; and in life, as in every thing elfe beheld at a diftance, there appears an even uniformity: the petty difcriminations which diverfify the natural character, are not difcoverable but by a clofe infpection; we, therefore, find them moft at home, becaufe there we have moft opportunities of remarking them. Much lefs am I convinced, that this peculiar diverfification, if it be real, is the confequence of peculiar liberty; for where is the government to be found that fuperintends individuals with fo much vigilance, as not to leave their private conduct without reftraint? Can it enter into a reafonable mind to imagine, that men of every other nation are not equally mafters of their own time or houfes with ourfelves, and equally at liberty to be parfimonious or profufe, frolic or fullen, abftinent or luxurious? Liberty is certainly neceffary to the full play of predominant humours; but fuch liberty is to be found alike under the government

7

of

of the many or the few, in monarchies or in commonwealths.

How readily the predominant paſſion ſnatches an interval of liberty, and how faſt it expands itſelf when the weight of reſtraint is taken away, I had lately an opportunity to diſcover, as I took a journey into the country in a ſtage coach ; which, as every journey is a kind of adventure, may be very properly related to you, though I can diſplay no ſuch extraordinary aſſembly as CERVANTES has collected at DON QUIXOTE's inn.

IN a ſtage-coach the paſſengers are for the moſt part wholly unknown to one another, and without expectation of ever meeting again when their journey is at an end ; one ſhould, therefore, imagine, that it was of little importance to any of them, what conjectures the reſt ſhould form concerning him.    Yet ſo it is, that as all think themſelves ſecure from detection, all aſſume that character of which they are moſt deſirous, and on no occaſion is the general ambition of ſuperiority more apparently indulged.

ON the day of our departure, in the twilight of the morning, I aſcended the vehicle with three men and two women, my fellow-travellers.    It was eaſy to obſerve the affected elevation of mien with which every one entered, and the ſupercilious civility with which they paid their compli-

ments

ments to each other. When the firſt ceremony was diſpatched, we ſat ſilent for a long time, all employed in collecting importance into our faces, and endeavouring to ſtrike reverence and ſubmiſſion into our companions.

It is always obſervable that ſilence propagates itſelf, and that the longer talk has been ſuſpended, the more difficult it is to find any thing to ſay. We began now to wiſh for converſation; but no one ſeemed inclined to deſcend from his dignity, or firſt propoſe a topic of diſcourſe. At laſt a corpulent gentleman, who had equipped himſelf for this expedition with a ſcarlet ſurtout and a large hat with a broad lace, drew out his watch, looked on it in ſilence, and then held it dangling at his finger. This was, I ſuppoſe, underſtood by all the company as an invitation to aſk the time of the day, but nobody appeared to heed his overture; and his deſire to be talking ſo far overcame his reſentment, that he let us know of his own accord that it was paſt five, and that in two hours we ſhould be at breakfaſt.

His condeſcenſion was thrown away; we continued all obdurate; the ladies held up their heads; I amuſed myſelf with watching their behaviour; and of the other two, one ſeemed to employ himſelf in counting the trees as we drove by them, the other drew his hat over his eyes and counterfeited a ſlumber. The man of benevolence, to shew that he was not depressed by our neglect, hummed a tune and beat time upon his snuff-box.

Thus universally displeased with one another, and not much delighted with ourselves, we came at last to the little inn appointed for our repast; and all began at once to recompense themselves for the constraint of silence, by innumerable questions and orders to the people that attended us. At last, what every one had called for was got, or declared impossible to be got at that time, and we were persuaded to sit round the same table; when the gentleman in the red surtout looked again upon his watch, told us that we had half an hour to spare, but he was sorry to see so little merriment among us; that all fellow-travellers were for the time upon the level, and that it was always his way to make himself one of the company. " I remember," says he, " it was on just such a morning as this, " that I and my lord Mumble and the duke of " Tenterden were out upon a ramble : we called " at a little house as it might be this; and my " landlady, I warrant you, not suspecting to " whom she was talking, was so jocular and fa- " cetious, and made so many merry answers to " our questions, that we were all ready to burst " with laughter. At last the good woman hap- " pening to overhear me whisper the duke and

" call

" call him by his title, was fo furprifed and
" confounded, that we could fcarcely get a word
" from her ; and the duke never met me from
" that day to this, but he talks of the little
" houfe, and quarrels with me for terrifying the
" landlady."

HE had fcarcely time to congratulate himfelf
on the veneration which this narrative muft have
procured him from the company, when one of
the ladies having reached out for a plate on a
diftant part of the table, began to remark " the
" inconveniences of travelling, and the difficulty
" which they who never fat at home without a
" great number of attendants found in perform-
" ing for themfelves fuch offices as the road
" required ; but that people of quality often
" travelled in difguife, and might be generally
" known from the vulgar by their condefcenfion
" to poor inn-keepers, and the allowance which
" they made for any defect in their entertain-
" ment ; that for her part, while people were
" civil and meant well, it was never her cuftom
" to find fault, for one was not to expect upon
" a journey all that one enjoyed at one's own
" houfe."

A GENERAL emulation feemed now to be excited. One of the men, who had hitherto faid
nothing, called for the laft news-paper ; and
having perufed it a while with deep penfivenefs,

" It

" It is impossible," says he, " for any man to " guess how to act with regard to the stocks : " last week it was the general opinion that they " would fall ; and I sold out twenty thousand " pounds in order to a purchase : they have now " risen unexpectedly ; and I make no doubt but " at my return to London I shall risk thirty " thousand pounds among them again."

A YOUNG man, who had hitherto distinguished himself only by the vivacity of his looks, and a frequent diversion of his eyes from one object to another, upon this closed his snuff-box, and told us, that " he had a hundred times talked with " the chancellor and the judges on the subject " of the stocks ; that for his part he did not " pretend to be well acquainted with the prin- " ciples on which they were established, but had " always heard them reckoned pernicious to " trade, uncertain in their produce, and unsolid " in their foundation ; and that he had been ad- " vised by three judges, his most intimate friends, " never to venture his money in the funds, but " to put it out upon land-security, till he could " light upon an estate in his own country."

IT might be expected, that upon these glimpses of latent dignity, we should all have began to look round us with veneration ; and have behaved like the princes of romance, when the enchantment that disguises them is dissolved, and

they

they difcover the dignity of each other : yet it happened, that none of thefe hints made much impreffion on the company; every one was apparently fufpected of endeavouring to impofe falfe appearances upon the reft; all continued their haughtinefs in hopes to enforce their claims; and all grew every hour more fullen, becaufe they found their reprefentations of them-felves without effect.

THUS we travelled on four days with malevo-lence perpetually increafing, and without any endeavour. but to outvie each other in fupercili-oufnefs and neglect; and when any two of us could feparate ourfelves for a moment, we vented our indignation at the faucinefs of the reft.

AT length the journey was at an end; and time and chance, that ftrip off all difguifes, have dif-covered, that the intimate of lords and dukes is a nobleman's butler, who has furnifhed a fhop with the money he has faved; the man who deals fo largely in the funds, is a clerk of a broker in 'Change-alley ; the lady who fo care-fully concealed her quality, keeps a cook-fhop behind the Exchange; and the young man, who is fo happy in the friendfhip of the judges, en-groffes and tranfcribes for bread in a garret of the Temple.  Of one of the women only I could make no difadvantageous detection, becaufe fhe had affumed no character, but accommodated

G 3                         herfelf

herself to the scene before her, without any struggle for diftinction or fuperiority.

I COULD not forbear to reflect on the folly of practifing a fraud, which, as the event shewed, had been already practised too often to fucceed, and by the fuccefs of which no advantage could have been obtained; of affuming a character, which was to end with the day; and of claiming upon falfe pretences honours which muft perifh with the breath that paid them.

BUT, Mr. ADVENTURER, let not thofe who laugh at me and my companions, think this folly confined to a ftage coach. Every man in the journey of life takes the fame advantage of the ignorance of his fellow-travellers, difguifes him-felf in counterfeited merit, and hears thofe praifes with complacency which his confcience re-proaches him for accepting. Every man deceives himfelf, while he thinks he is deceiving others; and forgets that the time is at hand when every illufion fhall ceafe, when fictitious excellence fhall be torn away, and ALL muft be fhown to, ALL in their real eftate.

T            I am, SIR,

Your humble fervant,

VIATOR.

NUMB. 85. TUESDAY, *August* 28, 1753.

*Qui cupit optatam cursu contingere metam,*
*Multa tulit fecitque puer.*　　　　HOR.

The youth, who hopes th' Olympic prize to
　　gain,
All arts muſt try, and every toil suſtain.

　　　　　　　　　　　　FRANCIS.

IT is obſerved by BACON, that " reading
" makes a full man, converſation a ready
" man, and writing an exact man."

　As BACON attained to degrees of knowledge
ſcarcely ever reached by any other man, the
directions which he gives for ſtudy have certainly
a juſt claim to our regard; for who can teach
an art with ſo great authority, as he that has
practiſed it with undiſputed ſucceſs ?

　UNDER the protection of ſo great a name, I
ſhall, therefore, venture to inculcate to my in-
genious contemporaries, the neceſſity of reading,
the fitneſs of conſulting other underſtandings than
their own, and of conſidering the ſentiments and
opinions of thoſe who, however neglected in the
preſent age, had in their own times, and many
of them a long time afterwards, ſuch reputation
for knowledge and acuteneſs, as will ſcarcely
ever be attained by thoſe that deſpiſe them.

AN

AN opinion has of late been, I know not how, propagated among us, that libraries are filled only with ufelefs lumber; that men of parts ftand in need of no affiftance; and that to fpend life in poring upon-books, is only to imbibe prejudices, to obftruct and embarrafs the powers of nature, to cultivate memory at the expence of judgment, and to bury reafon under a chaos of indigefted learning.

SUCH is the talk of many who think them-felves wife, and of fome who are thought wife by others; of whom part probably believe their own tenets, and part may be juftly fufpected of endeavouring to fhelter their ignorance in mul-titudes, and of wifhing to deftroy that reputation which they have no hopes to fhare. It will, I believe, be found invariably true, that learning was never decried by any learned man; and what credit can be given to thofe, who venture to condemn that which they do not know?

IF reafon has the power afcribed to it by its advocates, if fo much is to be difcovered by attention and meditation, it is hard to believe, that fo many millions, equally participating of the bounties of nature with ourfelves, have been for ages upon ages meditating in vain: if the wits of the prefent time expect the regard of po-fterity, which will then inherit the reafon which is now thought fuperior to inftruction, furely,
they

they may allow themfelves to be inftructed by the reafon of former generations. When, therefore, an author declares, that he has been able to learn nothing from the writings of his predecef-fors, and fuch a declaration has been lately made, nothing but a degree of arrogance unpardonable in the greateft human underftanding, can hinder him from perceiving that he is raifing prejudices againft his own performance; for with what hopes of fuccefs can he attempt that in which greater abilities have hitherto mifcarried? or with what peculiar force does he fuppofe himfelf invigorated, that difficulties hitherto invincible fhould give way before him?

Of thofe whom PROVIDENCE has qualified to make any additions to human knowledge, the number is extremely fmall; and what can be added by each fingle mind, even of this fuperior clafs, is very little: the greateft part of mankind muft owe all their knowledge, and all muft owe far the larger part of it, to the information of others. To underftand the works of celebrated authors, to comprehend their fyftems, and retain their reafonings, is a tafk more than equal to common intellects; and he is by no means to be accounted ufelefs or idle, who has ftored his mind with acquired knowledge, and can detail it occafionally to others who have lefs leifure or weaker abilities.

G 5 PERSIUS

PERSIUS has juftly obferved, that knowledge is nothing to him who is not known by others to poffefs it : to the fcholar himfelf it is nothing with refpect either to honour or advantage, for the world cannot reward thofe qualities which are concealed from it ; with refpect to others it is nothing, becaufe it affords no help to ignorance or error.

IT is with juftice, therefore, that in an ac-complifhed character, HORACE unites juft fen-timents with the power of expreffing them ; and he that has once accumulated learning, is next to confider, how he fhall moft widely diffufe and moft agreeably impart it.

A READY man is made by converfation. He that buries himfelf among his manufcripts " be-" fprent," as POPE expreffes it, " with learned " duft," and wears out his days and nights in perpetual refearch and folitary meditation, is too apt to lofe in his elocution what he adds to his wifdom ; and when he comes into the world, to appear overloaded with his own notions, like a man armed with weapons which he cannot wield. He has no facility of inculcating his fpeculations, of adapting himfelf to the various degrees of intellect which the accidents of converfation will prefent ; but will talk to moft unintelligibly, and to all unpleafantly.

I WAS

I WAS once prefent at the lectures of a profound philofopher, a man really fkilled in the
fcience which he profeffed, who having occafion
to explain the terms OPACUM and PELLUCIDUM,
told us, after fome hefitation, that OPACUM was,
as one might fay, OPAKE, and that PELLUCIDUM
fignified PELLUCID. Such was the dexterity
with which this learned reader facilitated to his
auditors the intricacies of fcience ; and fo true is
it, that a man may know what he cannot teach.

BOERHAAVE complains, that the writers who
have treated of chemiftry before him, are ufelefs
to the greater part of ftudents, becaufe they pre-
fuppofe their readers to have fuch degrees of fkill
as are not often to be found. Into the fame error
are all men apt to fall, who have familiarized
any fubject to themfelves in folitude : they difcourfe, as if they thought every other man had
been employed in the fame inquiries ; and expect that fhort hints and obfcure illufions will
produce in others, the fame train of ideas which
they excite in themfelves.

NOR is this the only inconvenience which the
man of ftudy fuffers from a reclufe life. When
he meets with an opinion that pleafes him, he
catches it up with eagernefs ; looks only after
fuch arguments as tend to his confirmation ; or
fpares himfelf the trouble of difcuffion, and
adopts it with very little proof ; indulges it long

G. 6                                    without

without fufpicion, and in time unites it to the general body of his knowledge, and treafures it up among inconteftible truths: but when he comes into the world among men who,. arguing upon diffimilar principles, have been led to different conclufions, and being placed in various fituations, view the fame object on many fides; he finds his darling pofition attacked, and himfelf in no condition to defend it: having thought always in one train, he is in the ftate of a man who having fenced always with the fame mafter, is perplexed and amazed by a new pofture of his antagonift; he is entangled in unexpected difficulties, he is haraffed by fudden objections, he is unprovided with folutions or replies, his furprize impedes his natural powers of reafoning, his thoughts are fcattered and confounded, and he gratifies the pride of airy petulance with an eafy victory.

It is difficult to imagine, with what obftinacy truths which one mind perceives almoft by intuition, will be rejected by another; and how many artifices muft be practifed, to procure admiffion for the moft evident propofitions into underftandings frighted by their novelty, or hardened againft them by accidental prejudice; it can fcarcely be conceived, how frequently, in thefe extemporaneous controverfies, the dull will be fubtile, and the acute abfurd; how often ftupidity

dity will elude the force of argument, by invol-
ving itfelf in its own gloom ; and miftaken in-
genuity will weave artful fallacies, which reafon
can fcarcely find means to difentangle.

In thefe encounters the learning of the reclufe ufually fails him : nothing but long habit
and frequent experiments can confer the power
of changing a pofition into various forms, pre-
fenting it in different points of view, connecting
it with known and granted truths, fortifying it
with intelligible arguments, and illuftrating it
by apt fimilitudes ; and he, therefore, that has
collected his knowledge in folitude, muft learn
its application by mixing with mankind.

But while the various opportunities of converfation invite us to try every mode of argument, and every art of recommending our fentiments, we are frequently betrayed to the ufe of
fuch as are not in themfelves ftrictly defenfible :
a man heated in talk, and eager of victory,
takes advantage of the miftakes or ignorance of
his adverfary, lays hold of conceffions to which
he knows he has no right, and urges proofs likely
to prevail on his opponent, though he knows
himfelf that they have no force : thus the feverity
of reafon is relaxed, many topics are accumulated, but without juft arrangement or diftinction ; we learn to fatisfy ourfelves with fuch
ratiocination as filences others ; and feldom recal

to a clofe examination, that difcourfe which
has gratified our vanity with victory and ap-
plaufe.

SOME caution, therefore, muft be ufed, leſt
copioufnefs and facility be made lefs valuable by
inaccuracy and confufion.   To fix the thoughts
by writing, and fubject them to frequent exami-
nations and reviews, is the beft method of en-
abling the mind to detect its own fophifms, and
keep it on guard againft the fallacies which it
practifes on others :  in converfation we naturally
diffufe our thoughts, and in writing we contract
them ; method is the excellence of writing, and
unconftraint the grace of converfation.

To read, write, and converfe in due propor-
tions, is, therefore, the bufinefs of a man of
letters.   For all thefe there is not often equal
opportunity ; excellence, therefore, is not often
attainable ; and moft men fail in one or other
of the ends propofed, and are full without readinefs, or ready without exactnefs.   Some defi-
ciency muft be forgiven all, becaufe all are men ;
and more muft be allowed to pafs uncenfured in
the greater part of the world, becaufe none can
confer upon himfelf abilities, and few have the
choice of fituations proper for the improvement
of thofe which nature has beftowed : it is, however, reafonable, to have PERFECTION in our
eye ;

VOL.III
Nº86.

The wandering wish of lawless
love Suppress ——

eye; that we may always advance towards it, though we know it never can be reached.

T

\*\*\*\*\*\*\*\*\*\*\*\*\*\*\*\*\*\*\*\*\*\*\*\*\*\*\*\*\*\*\*\*\*\*

NUMB. 86. SATURDAY, *September* 1, 1753.

*Concubitu prohibere vago.*——    HOR.'

The wandering wifh of lawlefs love fupprefs.
FRANCIS.

To the ADVENTURER.

SIR,

TO indulge that reftlefs impatience, which every man feels to relate incidents by which the paffions have been greatly affected, and communicate ideas that have been forcibly impreffed, I have given you fome account of my life, which, without farther apology or introduction, may, perhaps, be favourably received in an ADVENTURER.

MY mother died when I was very young; and my father, who was a naval commander, and had, therefore, no opportunity to fuperintend my conduct, placed me at a grammar fchool, and afterwards removed me to the univerfity.

At

At fchool the number of boys was fo great, that
to regulate our morals was impoffible; and at
the univerfity even my learning contributed to
the diffolutenefs of my manners. As I was an
only child, my father had always allowed me
more money than I knew how to lay out, otherwife than in the gratifrcation of my vices: I had
fometimes, indeed, been reftrained by a general
fenfe of right and wrong; but I now oppofed the
remonftrances of confcience by the cavils of fophiftry; and having learned of fome celebrated
philofophers, as well ancient as modern, to
prove that nothing is good but pleafure, I became a rake upon principle.

My father died in the fame year with queen
Anne, a few months before I became of age, and
left me a very confiderable fortune in the funds.
I immediately quitted the univerfity and came to
London, which I confidered as the great mart of
pleafure; and as I could afford to deal largely, I
wifely determined not to endanger my capital. I
projected a fcheme of life that was moft agreeable to my temper, which was rather fedate
than volatile, and regulated my expences with
the œconomy of a philofopher. I found that my
favourite appetites might be gratified with greater
convenience and lefs fcandal, in proportion as
my life was more private: inftead, therefore, of
incumbering myfelf with a family, I took the

firft

firſt floor of a houſe which was let into lodgings, hired one ſervant, and kept a brace of geldings at a livery ſtable. I conſtantly frequented the theatres, and found my principles confirmed by almoſt every piece that was repreſented, particularly my reſolution never to marry. In comedy, indeed, the action terminated in marriage; but it was generally the marriage of a rake, who gave up his liberty with reluctance, as the only expedient to recover a fortune; and the huſband and wife of the drama were wretches whoſe example juſtified this reluctance, and appeared to be exhibited for no other purpoſe than to warn mankind, that whatever may be preſumed by thoſe whom indigence has made deſperate, to marry is to forfeit the quiet, independence and felicity of life.

In this courſe I had continued twenty years, without having impaired my conſtitution, leſſened my fortune, or incumbered myſelf with an illegitimate offspring; when a girl about eighteen, juſt arrived from the country, was hired as a chambermaid by the perſon who kept the houſe in which I lodged: the native beauty of health and ſimplicity in this young creature, had ſuch an effect upon my imagination, that I practiſed every art to debauch her, and at length ſucceeded.

I FOUND

I FOUND it convenient for her to continue in the houfe, and, therefore, made no propofal of removing her into lodgings; but after a few months fhe found herfelf with child, a difcovery which interrupted the indolence of my fenfuality, and made me repent my indifcretion: however, as I would not incur my own cenfure by ingratitude or inhumanity, I provided her a lodging and attendants, and fhe was at length delivered of a daughter. The child I regarded as a new incumbrance; for though I did not confider myfelf as under parental or conjugal obligations, yet I could not think myfelf at liberty wholly to abandon either the mother or the infant. To the mother, indeed, I had ftill fome degree of inclination; though I fhould have been heartily content never to have feen her again, if I could at once have been freed from any farther trouble about her; but as fomething was to be done, I was willing to keep her within my reach, at leaft till fhe could be fubfervient to my pleafure no longer: the child, however, I would have fent away; but fhe intreated me to let her fuckle it, with an importunity which I could not refift. After much thinking, I placed her in a little fhop in the fuburbs, which I furnifhed, at the expence of about twenty pounds, with chandlery ware, commodities of which fhe had fome knowledge, as her father was a petty fhopkeeper

in

in the country: she reported that her husband had been killed in an engagement at sea, and that his pay, which she had been impowered to receive by his will, had purchased her stock. I now thought I had discharged every obligation, as I had enabled her to subsist, at least as well as she could have done by her labour in the station in which I found her; and as often as I had an inclination to see her, I sent for her to a bagnio.

BUT these interviews did not produce the pleasure which I expected: her affection for me was too tender and delicate; she often wept in spight of all her efforts against it; and could not forbear telling me stories of her little girl with the fond prolixity of a mother, when I wished to regard her only as a mistress. These incidents at once touched me with compunction, and quenched the appetite which I had intended to gratify; my visits, therefore, became less frequent: but she never sent after me when I was absent, nor reproached me, otherwise than by tears of tenderness when she saw me again.

AFTER the first year I wholly neglected her; and having heard nothing of her during the winter, I went to spend the summer in the country. When I returned, I was prompted rather by curiosity than desire to make some inquiry after her; and soon learnt that she had died

some

some months before of the small-pox, that the goods had been seized for rent, and the child taken by the parish. At this account, so sudden and unexpected, I was sensibly touched; and at first conceived a design to rescue the child from the hands of a parish nurse, and make some little provision for it when it should be grown up: but this was delayed from day to day, such was the supineness of my disposition, till the event was remembered with less and less sensibility; and at length I congratulated myself upon my deliverance from an engagement which I had always considered as resembling in some degree the shackles of matrimony. I resolved to incur the same embarrassment no more, and contented myself with strolling from one prostitute to another, of whom I had seen many generations perish; and the new faces which I once sought among the masks in the pit, I found with less trouble at Cuper's, Vauxhall, Ranelagh, and innumerable other places of public entertainment, which have appeared during the last twenty years of my life.

A FEW weeks ago I celebrated my sixtieth birth-day with some friends at a tavern; and as I was returning to my lodgings, I saw a hackney coach stop at the door of a house which I knew to be of ill repute, though it was private and of the first class. Just as I came up, a girl stepped

out

out of it, who appeared, by the imperfect glimpfe
I caught of her as fhe paffed, to be very young,
and extremely beautiful. As I was warm with
wine, I followed her in without hefitation, and
was delighted to find her equally charming upon
a nearer view. I detained the coach, and propofed that we fhould go to Haddock's : fhe hefi-
tated with fome appearance of unwillingnefs and
confufion, but at length confented : fhe foon
became more free, and I was not lefs pleafed
with her converfation than her perfon : I obferved that fhe had a foftnefs and modefty in her
manner, which is quickly worn off by habitual
proftitution.

WE had drank a bottle of French wine, and
were preparing to go to bed, when, to my unfpeakable confufion and aftonifhment, I difcovered a mark by which I knew her to be my
child : for I remembered, that the poor girl,
whom I fo cruelly feduced and neglected, had
once told me with tears in her eyes, that fhe had
imprinted the two letters of my name under her
little NANCY's left breaft, which, perhaps,
would be the only memorial fhe would ever have
of a father. I was inftantly ftruck with a fenfe
of guilt with which I had not been familiar;
and, therefore, felt all its force. The poor
wretch, whom I was about to hire for the gratification of a brutal appetite, perceived my diforder

order with furprife and concern : fhe enquired
with an officious folicitude, what fudden illnefs
had feized me ; fhe took my hand, preffed it,
and looked eagerly in my face, ftill inquifitive
what could be done to relieve me.   I remained
fome time torpid : but was foon rouzed by the
reflection, that I was receiving the careffes of my
child, whom I had abandoned to the loweft infamy, to be the flave of drunkennefs and luft,
and whom I had led to the brink of inceft.   I
fuddenly ftarted up ; firft held her at a diftance ;
then catching her in my arms, ftrove to fpeak,
but burft into tears.   I faw that fhe was confounded and terrified ; and as foon as I could
recover my fpeech, I put an end to her doubts
by revealing the fecret.

IT is impoffible to exprefs the effect it had
upon her : fhe ftood motionlefs a few minutes ;
then clafped her hands together, and looked up
in an agony, which not to have feen is not to
conceive.   The tears at length ftarted from her
eyes ; fhe recollected herfelf, called me father,
threw herfelf upon her knees, embracing mine,
and plunging a new dagger in my heart, by afk-
ing my bleffing.

WE fat up together the remainder of the night,
which I fpent in liftening to a ftory that I may,
perhaps, hereafter communicate ; and the next
day I took lodgings for her about fix miles from

town.

town. I visit her every day with emotions to which my heart has till now been a stranger, and which are every day more frequent and more strong. I propose to retire with her into some remote part of the country, and to atone for the past by the future : but, alas ! of the future a few years only can remain ; and of the past not a moment can return. What atonement can I make to those, upon whose daughters I have contributed to perpetuate that calamity, from which by miracle I have rescued my own ! How can I bear the reflection, that though for my own child I had hitherto expressed less kindness than brutes for their young ; yet, perhaps, every other whom I either hired or seduced to prostitution, had been gazed at in the ardor of parental affection, till tears have started to the eye ; had been catched to the bosom with transport, in the prattling simplicity of infancy ; had been watched in sickness with anxiety that suspended sleep ; had been fed by the toil of industrious poverty, and reared to maturity with hope and fear. What a monster is he, by whom these fears are verified, and this hope deceived ! And yet, so dreadful is the force of habitual guilt, I sometimes regret the restraint which is come upon me ; I wish to sink again into the slumber from which I have been rouzed, and to repeat the crimes which I abhor. My heart is this moment

ment burſting for utterance : but I want words.
Farewell.

                                AGAMUS.

NUMB. 87.   TUESDAY, *September* 4, 1753.

*Iracundior eſt paulò ; minùs aptus acutis*
*Naribus horum hominum ; rideri poſſit, ea quòd*
*Ruſticiùs tonſo toga defluit, & malè laxus*
*In pede calceus hæret :—at ingenium ingens*
*Inculto latet hoc ſub corpore——*        HOR.

Your friend is paſſionate ; perhaps unfit
For the briſk petulance of modern wit :
His hair ill cut, his robe that aukward flows,
Or his large ſhoes, to raillery expoſe
The man.——
But underneath this rough uncouth diſguiſe,
A genius of extenſive knowledge lies.

                                FRANCIS.

THERE are many accompliſhments, which
though they are comparatively trivial, and
may be acquired by ſmall abilities, are yet of
great importance in our common intercourſe with
men. Of this kind is that general courteſy,
which is called GOOD BREEDING ; a name, by
                                which,

which, as an artificial excellence, it is at once characterised and recommended.

GOOD Breeding, as it is generally employed in the gratification of vanity, a passion almost universally predominant, is more highly prized by the majority than any other; and he who wants it, though he may be preserved from contempt by incontestable superiority either of virtue or of parts, will yet be regarded with malevolence, and avoided as an enemy with whom it is dangerous to combat.

IN some instances, indeed, the enmity of others cannot be avoided without the participation of guilt; but then it is the enmity of those, with whom neither virtue nor wisdom can desire to associate: and good breeding may generally be practised upon more easy and more honourable terms, than acquiescence in the detraction of malice or the adulation of servility, the obscenity of a letcher or the blasphemy of an infidel. Disagreeable truths may be suppressed; and when they can be suppressed without guilt, they cannot innocently be uttered; the boast of vanity may be suffered without severe reprehension, and the prattle of absurdity may be heard without expressions of contempt.

IT happens, indeed, somewhat unfortunately, that the practice of good breeding, however necessary, is obstructed by the possession of more

valuable

valuable talents; and that great integrity, delicacy, fenfibility, and fpirit, exalted genius, and extenfive learning, frequently render men ill-bred.

PETRARCH relates, that his admirable friend and cotemporary, DANTE ALIGHERI, one of the moft exalted and original geniufes that ever appeared, being banifhed his country, and having retired to the court of a prince which was then the fanctuary of the unfortunate, was held at firft in great efteem; but became daily lefs acceptable to his patron, by the feverity of his manners and the freedom of his fpeech. There were at the fame court, many players and buffoons, gamefters and debauchees, one of whom, diftinguifhed by his impudence, ribaldry, and obfcenity, was greatly careffed by the reft; which the prince fufpecting DANTE not to be pleafed with, ordered the man to be brought before him, and having highly extolled him, turned to DANTE, and faid, "I wonder that this perfon, "who is by fome deemed a fool, and by others "a madman, fhould yet be fo generally pleaf- "ing, and fo generally beloved; when you, "who are celebrated for wifdom, are yet heard "without pleafure, and commended without "friendfhip." "You would ceafe to wonder," replied DANTE, "if you confidered, that a "conformity of character is the fource of "friendfhip."

" friendfhip." This farcafm, which had all the force of truth, and all the keennefs of wit, was intolerable; and DANTE was immediately difgraced and banifhed.

BUT by this anfwer, though the indignation which produced it was founded on virtue, DANTE probably gratified his own vanity, as much as he mortified that of others: it was the petulant reproach of refentment and pride, which is always retorted with rage; and not the fill voice of REASON, which is heard with complacency and reverence: if DANTE intended reformation, his anfwer was not wife; if he did not intend reformation, his anfwer was not good.

GREAT delicacy, fenfibility, and penetration, do not lefs obftruct the practice of good breeding than integrity. Perfons thus qualified, not only difcover proportionably more faults and failings in the characters which they examine, but are more difgufted with the faults and failings which they difcover: the common topics of converfation are too trivial to engage their attention; the various turns of fortune that have lately happened at a game at Whift, the hiftory of a ball at Tunbridge or Bath, a defcription of lady Fanny's jewels and lady Kitty's vapours, the journals of a horfe-race or a cock-match, and difquifitions on the game act or the fcarcity of partridges, are fubjects upon which men of delicate tafte do not always chufe to declaim, and on which they

H 2                    cannot

cannot patiently hear the declamation of others.
But they fhould remember, that their impatience
is the impotence of reafon and the prevalence of
vanity; that if they fit filent and referved,
wrapped up in the contemplation of their own
dignity, they will in their turn be defpifed and
hated by thofe whom they hate and defpife; and
with better reafon, for perverted power ought to
be more odious than debility. To hear with
patience, and to anfwer with civility, feems to
comprehend all the good breeding of converfation; and in proportion as this is eafy, filence
and inattention are without excufe.

He, who does not practife good breeding,
will not find himfelf confidered as the object of
good breeding by others. There is, however,
a fpecies of rufticity, which it is not lefs abfurd
than injurious to treat with contempt: this
fpecies of ill-breeding is become almoft pro-
verbially the characteriftic of a fcholar; nor
fhould it be expected, that he who is deeply
attentive to an abftrufe fcience, or who em-
ploys any of the three great faculties of the foul,
the memory, the imagination, or the judgment,
in the clofe purfuit of their feveral objects,
fhould have ftudied punctilios of form and ceremony, and be equally able to fhine at a route
and in the fchools. That the bow of a chrono-
loger, and the compliment of an aftronomer,
fhould be improper or uncouth, cannot be
thought

thought ſtrange to thoſe, who duly conſider the narrowneſs of our faculties, and the impoſſibility of attaining univerſal excellence.

EQUALLY excuſeable, for the ſame reaſons, are that abſence of mind, and that forgetfulneſs of place and perſon, to which ſcholars are ſo frequently ſubject.   When LEWIS XIV. was one day lamenting the death of an old comedian whom he highly extolled, " Yes," replied BOILEAU, in the preſence of madam MAINTE-NON, " he performed tolerably well in the deſ-" picable pieces of SCARRON, which are now " deſervedly forgotten even in the provinces."

As every condition of life, and every turn of mind, has ſome peculiar temptation and pro-penſity to evil, let not the man of uprightneſs and honeſty be moroſe and ſurly in his practice of virtue; let not him, whoſe delicacy and pene-tration diſcern with diſguſt thoſe imperfections in others from which he himſelf is not free, in-dulge perpetual peeviſhneſs and diſcontent; nor let learning and knowledge be pleaded as an ex-cuſe for not condeſcending to the common offices and duties of civil life : for as no man ſhould be WELL-BRED, at the expence of his VIRTUE ; no man ſhould practiſe virtue, ſo as to deter others from IMITATION.

Z

NUMB. 88.   SATURDAY, *September* 8, 1753.

———*Semperque relinqui*
*Sola fibi, femper longam incomitata videtur*
*Ire viam*———                     VIRG.

——— She feems alone,
To wander in her fleep, thro' ways unknown,
Guilelefs and dark.———       DRYDEN.

NEWTON, whofe power of inveftigat-
ing nature few will deny to have been
fuperior to their own, confeffes, that he cannot
account for gravity, the firft principle of his
fyftem, as a property communicable to matter ;
or conceive the phenomena fuppofed to be the
effects of fuch a principle, to be otherwife produced, than by the immediate and perpetual
influence of the ALMIGHTY : and, perhaps,
thofe who moft attentively confider the phenomena of the moral and natural world, will
be moft inclined to admit the agency of invifible
beings.

IN dreams, the mind appears to be wholly
paffive ; for dreams are fo far from being the
effect of a voluntary effort, that we neither
know of what we fhall dream, nor whether we
fhall dream at all.

THE human mind does not, indeed, appear
to have any power equal to fuch an effect ; for
the

the ideas conceived in dreams without the intervention of fensible objects, are much more perfect and ftrong than can be formed at other
times by the utmoft effort of the moft lively
imagination : and it can fcarce be fuppofed, that
the mind is more vigorous when we fleep, than
when we are awake; efpecially if it be true, as
I have before remarked, that "in fleep the
"power of memory is wholly fufpended, and
"the underftanding is employed only about
"fuch objects as prefent themfelves, without
"comparing the paft with the prefent;" except
we judge of the foul by a maxim which fome
deep philofophers have held concerning horfes,
that when the tail is cut off, the reft of the
members become more ftrong.

In lunacy, as in dreams, ideas are conceived
which material objects do not excite; and which
the force of imagination, exerted by a voluntary
effort, cannot form : but the mind of the lunatic,
befides being impreffed with the images of
things that do not fall under the cognizance of
his fenfes, is prevented from receiving correfponding images from thofe that do.  When the
vifionary monarch looks round upon his clothes
which he has decorated with the fpoils of his
bed, his mind does not conceive the ideas of rags
and ftraw, but of velvet, embroidery, and gold ;
and when he gazes at the bounds of his cell, the

H 4                              image

image impreſſed upon his mind is not that of a
naked wall which inclofes an area of ten feet
fquare; but of wainfcot, and painting, and
tapeſtry, the bounds of a fpacious apartment
adorned with magnificent furniture, and crowded with fplendid dependants.

Of the lunatic it is alfo univerfally true,
that his underſtanding is perverted to evils,
which a mere perverfion of the underftanding
does not neceſſarily imply; he either fits torpid
in defpair, or is bufied in the contrivance or
the execution of mifchief. But if lunacy is
ultimately produced by mere material caufes, it
is difficult to ſhew, why mifery or malevolence
ſhould always be complicated with abfurdity;
why madnefs ſhould not fometimes produce in-
ftances of frantic and extravagant kindnefs, of
a benevolent purpofe formed upon erroneous
principles and purfued by ridiculous means, and
of an honeft and harmlefs chearfulnefs arifing
from the fancied felicity of others.

A LUNATIC is, indeed, fometimes merry,
but the merry lunatic is never kind; his fport
is always mifchief; and mifchief is rather
aggravated than atoned by wantonnefs; his
difpofition is always evil in proportion to the
height of his phrenzy; and upon this occafion
it may be remarked, that if every approach to
madnefs is a deviation to ill, every deviation

to

to ill may be confidered as an approach to madnefs.

AMONG other unaccountable phenomena in lunacy, is the invincible abfurdity of opinion with refpeҫt to fome fingle objeҫt, while the mind operates with its full vigour upon every other: it fometimes happens, that when this objeҫt is prefented to the mind, reafon is thrown quite out of her feat, and the perverfion of the underftanding for a time becomes general; but fometimes it ftill continues to be perverted but in part, and the abfurdity itfelf is defended with all the force of regular argumentation.

A MOST extraordinary inftance of this kind may now be communicated to the public, without injury to a good man, or a good caufe which he fuccefsfully maintained.

MR. SIMON BROWNE, a diffenting teacher of exemplary life and eminent intellectual abilities, after having been fome time feized with melancholy, defifted from the duties of his function, and could not be perfuaded to join in any act of worfhip either public or private. His friends often urged him to account for this change in his conduct, at which they exprefled the utmoft grief and aftonifhment; and after much importunity he told them, " that he had fallen " under the fenfible difpleafure of GOD, who " had caufed his rational foul gradually to perifh,

" and left him only an animal life in common
" with brutes; that it was, therefore, prophane
" for him to pray, and incongruous to be pre-
" fent at the prayers of others."

IN this opinion, however abfurd, he was in-
flexible, at a time when all the powers of his
mind fubfifted in their full vigour, when his conceptions were clear, and his reafoning ftrong.

BEING once importuned to fay grace at the
table of a friend, he excufed himfelf many
times; but the requeft being ftill repeated, and
the company kept ftanding, he difcovered evident tokens of diftrefs, and after fome irrefolute
geftures and hefitation, expreffed with great fervor this ejaculation : " Moft merciful and al-
" mighty GOD, let thy fpirit, which moved
" upon the face of the waters when there was
" no light, defcend upon me; that from this
" darknefs there may rife up a man to praife
" thee !"

BUT the moft aftonifhing proof both of his
intellectual excellence and defect, is, " A de-
" fence of the RELIGION of NATURE and the
" CHRISTIAN REVELATION, in anfwer to
" Tindal's Chriftianity as old as the Creation,"
and his dedication of it to the late queen. The
book is univerfally allowed to be the beft which
that controverfy produced, and the dedication
is as follows :

" MADAM,

" MADAM,

" OF all the extraordinary things that have
" been tendered to your royal hands since
" your first happy arrival in Britain, it may be
" boldly said, what now bespeaks your majesty's
" acceptance is the chief.

" Not in itself indeed; it is a trifle un-
" worthy your exalted rank, and what will
" hardly prove an entertaining amusement to
" one of your majesty's deep penetration, exact
" judgment, and fine taste.

" But on account of the author, who is the
" first being of the kind, and yet without a
" name.

" He was once a man; and of some little
" name; but of no worth, as his present unpa-
" ralleled case makes but too manifest; for by
" the immediate hand of an avenging GOD,
" his very thinking substance has for more than
" seven years been continually wasting away,
" till it is wholly perished out of him, if it be
" not utterly come to nothing. None, no not
" the least remembrance of its very ruins, re-
" mains, not the shadow of an idea is left, nor
" any sense that, so much as one single one,
" perfect or imperfect, whole or diminished,
" ever did appear to a mind within him, or was
" perceived by it.

H 6

" Such

" SUCH a prefent from fuch a thing, however
" worthlefs in itfelf, may not be wholly unac-
" ceptable to your majefty, the author being
" fuch as hiftory cannot parallel : and if the
" fact, which is real and no fiction, nor wrong
" conccit, obtains credit, it muft be recorded
" as the moft memorable and indeed aftonifh-
" ing event in the reign of GEORGE the fecond,
" that a tract compofed by fuch a thing was
" prefented to the illuftrious CAROLINE; his
" royal confort needs not be added; fame, if
" I am not mifinformed, will tell that with
" pleafure to all fucceeding times.

" HE has been informed, that your majefty's
" piety is as genuine and eminent, as your ex-
" cellent qualities are great and confpicuous.
" This can, indeed, be truly known to the
" great fearcher of hearts only; HE alone, who
" can look into them, can difcern if they are
" fincere, and the main intention correfponds
" with the appearance; and your majefty can-
" not take it amifs, if fuch an author hints,
" that HIS fecret approbation is of infinitely
" greater value than the commendation of men,
" who may be eafily miftaken and are too apt to
" flatter their fuperiors.

" BUT if he has been told the truth, fuch a
" cafe as his will certainly ftrike your majefty
" with aftonifhment, and may raife that com-
" miferation

" miferation in your royal breaft which he has
" in vain endeavoured to excite in thofe of his
" friends ; who, by the moft unreafonable and
" ill-founded conceit in the world, have ima-
" gined, that a thinking being could for feven
" years together live a ftranger to its own powers,
" exercifes, operations and ftate, and to what the
" great God has been doing in it and to it.

" IF your majefty, in your moft retired ad-
" drefs to the KING of KINGS, fhould think of
" fo fingular a cafe, you may, perhaps, make it
" your devout requeft, that the reign of your
" beloved fovereign and confort may be renown-
" ed to all pofterity by the recovery of a foul
" now in the utmoft ruin, the reftoration of one
" utterly loft at prefent amongft men.

" AND fhould this cafe affect your royal breaft,
" you will recommend it to the piety and prayers
" of all the truly devout, who have the honour
" to be known to your majefty : many fuch
" doubtlefs there are ; though courts are not
" ufually the places where the devout refort, or
" where devotion reigns.　And it is not impro-
" bable, that multitudes of the pious through-
" out the land may take a cafe to heart, that
" under your majefty's patronage comes thus
" recommended.

" COULD fuch a favour as this reftoration be
" obtained from HEAVEN by the prayers of
" your

" your majesty, with what a tranfport of grati-
" tude would the recovered being throw himfelf
" at your majesty's feet, and adoring the DIVINE
" POWER and GRACE, profefs himfelf,

    " MADAM,

        " Your majesty's moft obliged
            " and dutiful fervant."

THIS dedication, which is no where feeble
or abfurd, but in the places where the object of
his phrenzy was immediately before him, his
friends found means to fupprefs; wifely confidering, that a book, to which it fhould be prefixed, would certainly be condemned without
examination; for few would have required
ftronger evidence of its inutility, than that the
author, by his dedication, appeared to be mad.
The copy, however, was preferved, and has
been tranfcribed into the blank leaves before one
of the books which is now in the library of a
friend to this undertaking, who is not lefs diftinguifhed by his merit than his rank, and who
recommended it as a literary curiofity, which
was in danger of being loft for want of a repo-
fitory in which it might be preferved.

NUMB. 89. TUESDAY, *September* 11, 1753.

*Præcipua tamen ejus in commovendâ miferatione
virtus, ut quidam in hac eum parte omnibus ejufdem
operis autoribus præferant.* QUINTILIAN.

His great excellence was in moving compaſſion, with reſpect to which many give him the
firſt place of all the writers of that kind.

To the ADVENTURER.

SIR,

IT is uſual for ſcholars to lament, with indiſ-
criminating regret, the devaſtations committed on ancient libraries, by accident and time,
by ſuperſtition, ignorance, and gothiciſm : but
the loſs is very far from being in all caſes equally
irreparable, as the want of ſome kinds of books
may be much more eaſily ſupplied than that of
others. By the interruption that ſometimes happens in the ſucceſſion of philoſophical opinions,
the mind is emancipated from traditionary ſyſ-
tems, recovers its native elaſticity which had
been benumbed by cuſtom, begins to examine
with freedom and freſh vigour, and to follow
truth inſtead of authority. The loſs of writings,
therefore, in which reaſoning is concerned, is
not,

not, perhaps, fo great an evil to mankind, as of thofe which defcribe characters and facts.

To be deprived of the laft books of LIVY, of the fatires of ARCHILOCHUS, and the comedies of MENANDER, is a greater misfortune to the republic of literature, than if the logic and the phyfics of ARISTOTLE had never defcended to pofterity.

Two of your predeceffors, Mr. ADVENTURER, of great judgment and genius, very juftly thought that they fhould adorn their lucubrations by publifhing, one of them a fragment of SAPPHO, and the other an old Grecian hymn to the Goddefs HEALTH: and, indeed, I conceive it to be a very important ufe of your paper, to bring into common light thofe beautiful remains of ancient art, which by their prefent fituation are deprived of that univerfal admiration they fo juftly deferve, and are only the fecret enjoyment of a few curious readers. In imitation, therefore, of the examples I have juft mentioned, I fhall fend you, for the inftruction and entertainment of your readers, a fragment of SIMONIDES and of MENANDER.

SIMONIDES was celebrated by the ancients for the fweetnefs, correctnefs, and purity of his ftyle, and his irrefiftible fkill in moving the paffions. It is a fufficient panegyric that PLATO often mentions him with approbation. DIONYSIUS places

him.

him among thofe polifhed writers, who excel
" in a fmooth volubility, and flow on, like
" plenteous and perennial rivers, in a courfe of
" even and uninterrupted harmony."

IT is to this excellent critic that we are indebted for the prefervation of the following paffage, the tendernefs and elegance of which
fcarcely need be pointed out to thofe who have
tafte and fenfibility. DANAË, being by her
mercilefs father inclofed in a cheft and thrown
into the fea with her child, the poet proceeds
thus far to relate her diftrefs:

Ὅτε λάρυακι ἐν δαιδαλέα ἄνεμ☉
Βρέμη πνίων, κινηθεῖσα δὲ λίμνα
Δείματι ἔρειπεν· ὔτ' ἀδιάνταισι
Παρειαῖς, ἀμφὶ τὲ Περσεῖ βάλλε
Φίλαν χέρα εἶπέν τε———Ὦ τέκνον,
Οἷον ἔχω, πόνον. σὺ δ' αὖτε γαλαθηνῷ
Ἥτορι κνώσσεις ἐν ἀτερπεῖ δώματι,
Χαλχεογόμφῳ δὲ, νυκτιλαμπεῖ,
Κυανέῳ τὲ δνόφῳ. σὺ δ', αὐαλέαν
Ὕπερθε τεὰν κόμαν βαθεῖαν
Παρίοντος κύματ☉ ὐκ ἀλέγεις
Οὐδ' ἀνέμκ φθόγγων, πορθυρέᾳ
Κείμενος ἐν χλανίδι, πρόσωπον καλὸν,
Εἰ δὲ τοὶ δεινὸν τό γε δεινὸν ἦν,
Καὶ κὲν ἐμῶν ῥημάτων λεπίον
Ὑπεῖχες ὔας. Κέλομαι, εὖδε βρέφ☉,
Εὑδέτω δὲ πόνῖος, εὑδέτω ἄμειρον κακὸν.

WHEN

WHEN the raging wind began to roar, and the waves to beat so violently on the chest as to threaten to overset it, she threw her arm fondly around PERSEUS, and said, the tears trickling down her cheeks, " O my son, what sorrows " do I undergo ! But thou art wrapt in a deep " slumber ; thou sleepest soundly like a sucking " child, in this joyless habitation, in this dark " and dreadful night, lighted only by the glim- " merings of the moon ! Covered with thy " purple mantle, thou regardest not the waves " that dash around thee, nor the whistling of " the winds. O thou beauteous babe ! If thou " wert sensible of this calamity, thou wouldest " bend thy tender ears to my complaints. Sleep " on, I beseech thee, O my child ! Sleep, with " him, O ye billows ! and sleep likewise my " distress !"

THOSE who would form a full idea of the delicacy of the Greek, should attentively con- sider the following happy imitation of it, which, I have reason to believe, is not so extensively known or so warmly admired as it ought to be ; and which, indeed, far excels the original.

THE poet, having pathetically painted a great princess taking leave of an affectionate husband on his death-bed, and endeavouring afterwards to comfort her inconsolable family, adds the following particular.

*His*

His conatibus occupata, ocellos
Guttis lucidulis adhuc madentes
Convertit, puerum sopore vinctum
Quà nutrix placido sinû fovebat :
" Dormis," inquiit, " O miselle, nec te
" Vultus exanimes, silentiumque
" Per longa atria commovent, nec ullo
" Fratrum tangeris, aut meo dolore ;
" Nec sentis patre destitutus illo,
" Qui gestans genibusve brachieve,
" Aut formans lepidam tuam loquelam,
" Tecum mille modis ineptiebat.
" Tu dormis, volitantque qui solebant
" Risus, in roseis tuis labellis.———
" Dormi, parvule ! nec mali dolores
" Qui matrem cruciant tuæ quietis
" Rumpant somnia.—Quando, quando, tales
" Redibunt oculis meis sopores !"

The contrast betwixt the insensibility of the infant and the agony of the mother ; her observing
that the child is unmoved with what was most
likely to affect him, the sorrows of his little
brothers, the many mournful countenances,
and the dismal silence that reigned throughout
r                                                    the

the court ; the circumſtances of the father play-
ing with the child on his knees or in his arms,
and teaching him to ſpeak ; are ſuch delicate
maſter-ſtrokes of nature and parental tenderneſs, as ſhew the author is intimately acquainted
with the human heart, and with thoſe little
touches of paſſion that are beſt calculated to
move it.    The affectionate wiſh of " dormi,
" parvule !" is plainly imitated from the fragment of SIMONIDES ; but the ſudden exclamation that follows,—" when, O when, ſhall I
" ſleep like this infant !" is entirely the property
of the author, and worthy of, though not excelled by, any of the ancients.   It is making the
moſt artful and the moſt ſtriking uſe of the
ſlumber of the child, to aggravate and heighten
by compariſon the reſtleſſneſs of the mother's
ſorrow ; it is the fineſt and ſtrongeſt way of ſaying, " my grief will never ceaſe," that has ever
been uſed.   I think it not exaggeration to affirm,
that in this little poem are united the pathetic of
EURIPIDES and the elegance of CATULLUS.
It affords a judicious example of the manner in
which the ancients ought to be imitated ; not
by uſing their expreſſions and epithets, which is
the common method, but by catching a portion
of their ſpirit, and adapting their images and
ways of thinking to new ſubjects.    The generality of thoſe who have propoſed CATULLUS
for

for their pattern, even the beſt of the modern
Latin poets of Italy, ſeem to think they have
accompliſhed their deſign, by introducing many
florid diminutives, ſuch as " tenellula, and
" columbula:" but there is a purity and ſeverity
of ſtile, a temperate and auſtere manner in CA-
TULLUS, which nearly reſembles that of his
cotemporary LUCRETIUS, and is happily copied
by the author of the poem which has produced
theſe reflections.   Whenever, therefore, we ſit
down to compoſe, we ſhould aſk ourſelves in the
words of LONGINUS a little altered; " How
" would HOMER or PLATO, DEMOSTHENES
" or THUCYDIDES, have expreſſed themſelves
" on this occaſion; allowing for the alteration
" of our cuſtoms, and the different idioms of
" our reſpective languages?" This would be
following the ancients, without tamely treading
in their footſteps; this would be making the
ſame glorious uſe of them that RACINE has done
of EURIPIDES in his PHÆDRA and IPHIGENIA,
and that MILTON has done of the PROMETHEUS
of ESCHYLUS in the character of SATAN.

IF you ſhould happen not to lay aſide this
paper among the refuſe of your correſpondence,
as the offspring of pedantry and a blind fondneſs
for antiquity; or rather, if your readers can endure the ſight of ſo much Greek, though ever ſo
ATTIC; I may, perhaps, trouble you again
with

with a few reflections on the character of ME-
NANDER.

Z          I am,
              Mr. ADVENTURER,
                    Yours,

                          PALÆOPHILUS.


\*\*\*\*\*\*\*\*\*\*\*\*\*\*\*\*\*\*\*\*\*\*\*\*\*\*\*\*\*\*\*


NUMB. 90.  SATURDAY, *September* 15, 1753.

*Concretam exemit labem, purumque reliquit*
*Ætherium sensum, atque auraï simplicis ignem.*
                                        VIRGIL.

————By length of time,
The scurf is worn away of each committed
    crime;
No speck is left of their habitual stains,
But the pure æther of the soul remains.
                                        DRYDEN.


To the ADVENTURER.

SIR,

NOTHING sooner quells the ridiculous
triumph of human vanity, than reading
those passages of the greatest writers, in which
                                        they

they feem deprived of that noble fpirit that in-
fpires them in other parts; and where, inftead
of invention and grandeur, we meet with nothing but flatnefs and infipidity.

THE pain I have felt in obferving a lofty
genius thus fink beneath itfelf, has often made
me wifh, that thefe unworthy ftains could be
blotted from their works, and leave them perfect
and immaculate.

I WENT to bed a few nights ago, full of thefe
thoughts, and clofed the evening, as I frequently
do, with reading a few lines in VIRGIL.   I accidentally opened that part of the fixth book,
where ANCHISES recounts to his fon the various
methods of purgation which the foul undergoes
in the next world, to cleanfe it from the filth
it has contracted by its connection with the
body, and to deliver the pure etherial effence
from the vicious tincture of mortality.   This
was fo much like my evening's fpeculation, that
it infenfibly mixed and incorporated with it,
and as foon as I fell afleep, formed itfelf into
the following dream.

I FOUND myfelf in an inftant in the midft of
a temple which was built with all that magnificent fimplicity that diftinguifhes the productions
of the ancients.   At the eaft end was raifed an
altar, on each fide of which ftood a prieft, who
feemed preparing to facrifice.   On the altar was
                                            kindled

kindled a fire, from which arofe the brighteſt flame I had ever beheld. The light which it difpenfed, though remarkably ſtrong and clear, was not quivering and dazzling, but ſteady and uniform, and diffuſed a purple radiance through the whole edifice, not unlike the firſt appearance of the morning.

WHILE I ſtood fixed in admiration, my attention was awakened by the blaſt of a trumpet that ſhook the whole temple; but it carried a certain ſweetneſs in its found, which mellowed and tempered the natural ſhrillneſs of that inſtrument. After it had founded thrice, the being who blew it, habited according to the defcription of FAME by the ancients, iſſued a proclamation to the following purpofe: "By command of "APOLLO and the MUSES, all who have ever "made any pretenſions to fame by their "writings, are enjoined to facrifice upon the "altar in this temple, thofe parts of their "works, which have hitherto been preferved "to their infamy, that their names may "defcend fpotlefs and unfullied to poſterity. "For this purpofe ARISTOTLE and LON- "GINUS are appointed chief prieſts, who "are to fee that no improper oblations are "made, and no proper ones concealed; and "for the more eafy performance of this office, "they are allowed to chufe as their aſſiſtants "whomfoever

" whomsoever they shall think worthy of the
" function." ·

As soon as this proclamation was made,
I turned my eyes with inexpressible delight towards the two priests; but was soon robbed of
the pleasure of looking at them by a crowd of
people running up to offer their service. These
I found to be a groupe of French critics; but
their offers were rejected by both priests with
the utmost indignation, and their whole works
were thrown on the altar, and reduced to ashes
in an instant. The two priests then looked
round, and chose, with a few others, HORACE
and QUINTILIAN from among the Romans,
and ADDISON from the English, as their principal assistants.

THE first who came forward with his offering,
by the loftiness of his demeanor was soon difcovered to be HOMER. He approached the
altar with great majesty, and delivered to LON-
GINUS those parts of his ODYSSEY, which have
been censured as improbable fictions, and the ridiculous narratives of old age. LONGINUS was
preparing for the sacrifice, but observing that
ARISTOTLE did not seem willing to assist him in
the office, he returned them to the venerable old
bard with great deference, saying, that " they
" were indeed the tales of old age, but it was
" the old age of HOMER."

VIRGIL appeared next, and approached the altar with a modeſt dignity in his gait and countenance peculiar to himſelf; and to the ſurpriſe of all committed his whole ÆNEID to the flames. But it was immediately reſcued by two Romans, whom I found to be TUCCA and VARIUS, who ran with precipitation to the altar, delivered the poem from deſtruction, and carried off the author between them, repeating that, glorious boaſt of about forty lines at the beginning of the third Georgic :

> ————*Tentanda via eſt ; qua me quoque poſſim Tollere humo, victorque virûm volitare per ora, Primus ego in patriam mecum,* &c.

AFTER him moſt of the Greek and Roman authors proceeded to the altar, and ſurrendered with great modeſty and humility the moſt faulty part of their works. One circumſtance was obſervable, that the ſacrifice always increaſed in proportion as the author had ventured to deviate from a judicious imitation of HOMER. The latter Roman authors, who ſeemed almoſt to have loſt ſight of him, made ſo large offerings, that ſome of their works, which were before very voluminous, ſhrunk into the compaſs of a primer.

IT

It gave me the highest satisfaction to see Philosophy thus cleared from erroneous principles, History purged of falsehood, Poetry of fustian, and nothing left in each but Genius, Sense, and Truth.

I marked with particular attention the several offerings of the most eminent English writers. Chaucer gave up his obscenity, and then delivered his works to Dryden, to clear them from the rubbish that encumbered them. Dryden executed his task with great address, " and," as Addison says of Virgil in his Georgics, " tossed about his dung with " an air of gracefulness :" he not only repaired the injuries of time, but threw in a thousand new graces. He then advanced towards the altar himself, and delivered up a large pacquet, which contained many plays, and some poems. The pacquet had a label affixed to it, which bore this inscription, " To Poverty."

Shakespeare carried to the altar a long string of puns, marked " The Taste of the " Age," a small parcel of bombast, and a pretty large bundle of incorrectness. Notwithstanding the ingenuous air with which he made this offering, some officiates at the altar accused him of concealing certain pieces, and mentioned the London Prodigal, Sir Thomas Cromwell, The Yorkshire Tragedy, &c. The poet replied,

" that

" that as thofe pieces were unworthy to be pre-
" ferved, he fhould fee them confumed to afhes
" with great pleafure: but that he was wholly
" innocent of their original." The two chief
priefts interpofed in this difpute, and difmiffed
the poet with many compliments; LONGINUS
obferving, that the pieces in queftion could not
poffibly be his, for that the failings of SHAKE-
SPEARE were like thofe of HOMER, " whofe ge-
" nius, whenever it fubfided, might be compared
" to the ebbing of the ocean, which left a mark
" upon its fhores, to fhew to what a height it
" was fometimes carried." ARISTOTLE concurred in this opinion, and added, " that although
" SHAKESPEARE was quite ignorant of that ex-
" act œconomy of the ftage, which is fo re-
" markable in the Greek writers, yet the meer
" ftrength of his genius had in many points
" carried him infinitely beyond them."

MILTON gave up a few errors in his PARA-
DISE LOST, and the facrifice was attended
with great decency by ADDISON. OTWAY
and ROWE threw their comedies upon the altar,
and BEAUMONT and FLETCHER the two laft
acts of many of their pieces. They were followed by TOM DURFEY, ETHEREGE, WY-
CHERLEY, and feveral other dramatic writers,
who made fuch large contributions, that they
fet the altar in a blaze.

AMONG

·AMONG thefe I was furprifed to fee an author with much politenefs in his behaviour, and fpirit in his countenance, tottering under an unwieldy burden. As he approached I difcovered him to be Sir JOHN VANBRUGH, and could not but fmile, when, on his committing his heavy load to the flames, it proved to be " His fkill in Architecture."

POPE advanced towards ADDISON, and delivered with great humility thofe lines written exprefsly againft him, fo remarkable for their excellence and their cruelty, repeating this couplet;

" Curft be the verfe, how well foe'er it flow,
" That tends to make one worthy man my foe."

THE ingenuous critic infifted on his taking them again : " for," faid he, " my affociates " at the altar, particularly HORACE, would " never permit a line of fo excellent a fatirift " to be confumed. The many compliments " paid me in other parts of your works, am- " ply compenfate for this flight indignity. " And be affured, that no little pique or mif- " underftanding fhall ever make me a foe to " genius." POPE bowed in fome confufion, and promifed to fubftitute a fictitious name at leaft, which was all that was left in his power. He then retired, after having made a facrifice

of

of a little pacquet of Antithefes, and fome parts
of his Tranflation of Homer.

DURING the courfe of thefe oblations, I was
charmed with the candour, decency, and judge-
ment, with which all the priefts difcharged their
different functions.   They behaved with fuch
dignity, that it reminded me of thofe ages, when
the offices of king and prieft centered in the
fame perfon.   Whenever any of the affiftants
were at a lofs in any particular circumftances,
they applied to ARISTOTLE, who fettled the
whole bufinefs in an inftant.

BUT the reflections which this pleafing fcene
produced, were foon interrupted by a tumultuous noife at the gate of the temple; when
fuddenly a rude illiterate multitude rufhed in,
led by TINDAL, MORGAN, CHUBB, and BO-
LINGBROKE.   The chiefs, whofe countenances were impreffed with rage which art
could not conceal, forced their way to the altar, and amidft the joyful acclamations of their
followers threw a large volume into the fire.
But the triumph was fhort, and joy and accla-
mation gave way to filence and aftonifhment:
the volume lay unhurt in the midft of the fire,
and, as the flames played innocently about it,
I could difcover written in letters of gold, the
words, THE BIBLE.   At that inftant my
ears were ravifhed with the found of more than

mortal

mortal mufic accompanying a hymn fung by invifible beings, of which I well remember the following verfes :

" THE words of the LORD are pure words : " even as the filver, which in the earth is tried, " and purified feven times in the fire.

" MORE to be defired are they than gold ; " yea, than much fine gold : fweeter alfo than " honey, and the honey-comb."

THE united melody of inftruments and voices, which formed a concert fo exquifite, that, as MILTON fays, " it might create a foul " under the ribs of death," threw me into fuch extafies, that I was awakened by their violence.

&

I am, SIR,

Your humble fervant,

CRITO.

I 4

NUMB. 91.  TUESDAY, *September* 18, 1753.

———*Facto pius et sceleratus eodem.*    OVID.

Thus was the father pious to a crime.

ADDISON.

IT is contended by those who reject CHRI-
STIANITY, that if revelation had been neceffary as a rule of life to mankind, it would
have been univerfal; and they are, upon this
principle, compelled to affirm that only to be a
rule of life, which is univerfally known.

But no rule of life is univerfally known, except the dictates of confcience. With refpect to
particular actions, opinion determines whether
they are good or ill; and confcience approves
or difapproves, in confequence of this determination, whether it be in favour of truth or falfehood. Nor can the errors of confcience be always imputed to a criminal neglect of inquiry:
thofe, by whom a fyftem of moral truths was
difcovered through the gloom of paganifm, have
been confidered as prodigies, and regarded by
fucceffive ages with aftonifhment and admiration; and that which immortalifed one among
many millions, can fcarce be thought poffible to
all. Men do not ufually fhut their eyes againft
their immediate intereft, however they may be
                                    thought

thought to wink againſt their duty; and ſo little does either appear to be diſcoverable by the light of nature, that where the DIVINE PRESCRIP-TION has either been with-held or corrupted, ſuperſtition has rendered piety cruel, and error has armed virtue againſt herſelf; miſery has been cultivated by thoſe who have not incurred guilt; and though all men had been innocent, they might ſtill have been wretched.

IN the reign of YAMODIN the Magnificent, the kingdom of Golconda was depopulated by a peſtilence; and after every other attempt to propitiate the gods had failed, it was believed, according to the ſuperſtition of the country, that they required the ſacrifice of a virgin of royal blood.

IT happened that at this time there was no virgin of the royal blood, but TAMIRA the daughter of YAMODIN, whom he had betrothed to one of the princes of his court, intending that he ſhould ſucceed to the throne; for YAMODIN had no ſon, and he was not willing that his empire ſhould deſcend to a woman.

YAMODIN conſidered himſelf net leſs the father of his people, than of TAMIRA; and, therefore, with whatever reluctance, determined to redeem the life of the public, with that of the individual. He proſtrated himſelf in the temple, and invoked his principal idol as the fountain of

life:

life : " from thee," faid he, " I have derived
" my being, and the life which I have propa-
" gated is thine : when I am about to reſtore
" it, let me remember with gratitude, that I
" poſſeſſed it by thy bounty; and let thy mercy
" accept it as a ranſom for my people."

ORDERS were given for the ſacrifice on the
next day, and TAMIRA was permitted to diſpoſe of the interval as ſhe pleaſed.   She received
the intimation of her father's pleaſure without
much ſurprize; becauſe, as ſhe knew the cuſtom
of her country, ſhe ſcarce hoped that the demand of her life would have been delayed ſo
long : ſhe fortified herſelf againſt the terrors of
death, by anticipating the honours that would
be paid to her memory ; and had juſt triumphed
over the deſire of life, when, upon perceiving
her lover enter the apartment, ſhe loſt her fortitude in a moment and burſt into tears.

WHEN they were alone, after his eyes had,
like her's, overflowed with ſilent ſorrow, he took
her hand, and with a look of inexpreſſible anxiety
and tenderneſs told her, that one expedient was
yet left, by which her life might be preſerved ;
that he had bribed a prieſt to his intereſt, by
whom the ceremonies of marriage might be immediately performed ; that on the morrow, as
ſhe would be no longer a virgin, the propitiation
of the gods could not be effected by her death ;

and

and that her father, though for political purpofes he might appear to be difpleafed, would
yet fecretly rejoice at an event, which, without
his concurrence, had delivered him from the
dreadful obligation of facrificing an only child,
through whom he hoped to tranfmit dominion
to his pofterity.

To this propofal TAMIRA, whofe attachment
to life was now ftrengthened by love, and in
whofe bofom the regret of precluded pleafure had
fucceeded to the hope of glory, at length confented ; but fhe confented with all the timidity,
reluctance, and confufion, which are produced
by a confcioufnefs of guilt ; and the prince himfelf introduced the man, who was to accomplifh
the purpofe both of his ambition and his love,
with apparent tremor and hefitation.

On the morrow, when the prieft ftood ready
at the altar to receive the victim, and the king
commanded his daughter to be brought forth,
the prince produced her as his wife. YAMODIN
ftood fome moments in fufpence ; and then difmiffing the affembly, retired to his palace. After
having remained about two hours in private, he
fent for the prince. " The gods," faid he,
" though they continue the peftilence, have
" yet in mercy refcued my people from the op-
" preffion of a tyrant, who appears to confider
" the life of millions as nothing in competition

" with

" with the indulgence of his luft, his avarice,
" or his ambition." YAMODIN then commanded him to be put to death, and the fentence
was executed the fame hour.

TAMIRA now repented in unutterable diftrefs
of a crime, by which the pleafures not only of
poffeffion but hope were precluded; her attachment to life was broken, by the very means
which fhe had taken to preferve it; and as an
atonement for the forfeit of her virginity, fhe
determined to fubmit to that law of marriage,
from which as a princefs only fhe was exempted,
and to throw herfelf on the pile by which the
body of her hufband was to be confumed. To
this her father confented: their afhes were fcattered to the winds, and their names were forbidden to be repeated.

IF by thefe events it is evident, that YAMODIN
difcerned no law which would have juftified the
prefervation of his daughter; and if it is abfurd
to fuppofe his integrity to be vicious, becaufe
he had lefs power and opportunity to obtain
knowledge than PLATO; it will follow, that,
by whatever rule the oblation of human facrifice
may be condemned, the conduct of YAMODIN
which would have produced fuch facrifice was
morally right, and that of the prince which prevented it was morally wrong; that the confent
of TAMIRA to the marriage was vicious, and
that

that her fuicide was heroic virtue, though in her marriage fhe concurred with a general law of nature, and by her death oppofed it : for moral right and wrong are terms that are wholly relative to the agent by whom the action is performed, and not to the action itfelf confidered abstract-edly, for abstractedly it can be right or wrong only in a natural fenfe.   It appears, therefore, that REVELATION is neceffary to the eftablifh-ment even of natural religion, and that it is more rational to fuppofe it has been vouchfafed in part than not at all.

IT may, perhaps, be afked, of what ufe then is confcience as a guide of life, fince in thefe inftan-ces it appears not to coincide with the DIVINE LAW, but to oppofe it ; to condemn that which is enjoined, and approve that which is forbidden : but to this queftion the anfwer is eafy.

THE end which confcience approves is al-ways good, though fhe fometimes miftakes the means : the end which YAMODIN propofed, was deliverance from a peftilence ; but he did not nor could know, that this end was not to be obtained by human facrifice : and the end which confcience condemns, is always ill ; for the end propofed by the prince, was private gain by pub-lic lofs.  By confcience, then, all men are re-ftrained from intentional ill, and directed in their choice of the end though not of the means : it

infallibly

infallibly directs us to avoid guilt, but is not intended to fecure us from error ; it is not, therefore, either ufelefs as a law to ourfelves, nor
yet fufficient to regulate our conduct with refpect
to others ; it may fting with remorfe, but it cannot chear us with hope.    It is by REVELATION
alone, that virtue and happinefs are connected :
by REVELATION, " we are led into all truth ;"
confcience is directed to effect its purpofe, and
repentance is encouraged by the hope of pardon.
If this fun is rifen upon our hemifphere, let us
not confider it only as the object of fpeculation
and inquiry ; let us rejoice in its influence, and
walk by its light ; regarding rather with contempt
than indignation, thofe who are only follicitous
to difcover, why its radiance is not farther diffufed ; and wilfully fhut their eyes againft it,
becaufe they fee others ftumble to whom it has
been denied.

IT is not neceffary to inquire, what would be
determined at the GREAT TRIBUNAL, concerning a heathen who had in every inftance obeyed
the dictates of confcience, however erroneous ;
becaufe it will readily be granted, that no fuch
moral perfection was ever found among men :
but it is eafy to afcertain the fate of thofe, " who
" love darknefs rather than light, becaufe their
" deeds are evil ;" who violate the law that has
been written upon the heart, and reject that
                                              which

which has been offered them from ABOVE; who
though their sins are as scarlet, cavil at the terms
on which they might be white as snow; and
though their iniquities have been multiplied
without number, revile the hand that would
blot them from the REGISTER of HEAVEN.

✳✳✳✳✳✳✳✳✳✳✳✳✳✳✳✳✳✳✳✳✳✳✳✳✳✳✳✳✳✳✳✳✳✳

NUMB. 92.   SATURDAY, *September* 22, 1753.

*Cum tabulis animum censoris sumet honesti.*

HOR.

Bold be the critic, zealous to his trust,
Like the firm judge inexorably just.

To the ADVENTURER.

SIR,

IN the papers of criticism which you have
given to the public, I have remarked a spirit
of candor and love of truth, equally remote
from bigotry and captiousness; a just distribution
of praise amongst the ancients and the moderns;
a sober deference to reputation long established,
without a blind adoration of antiquity; and a
willingness to favour later performances, without a light or puerile fondness for novelty.

I SHALL, therefore, venture to lay before
you, such observations as have risen to my mind
in

in the confideration of VIRGIL's paftorals, without any inquiry how far my fentiments deviate from eftablifhed rules or common opinions.

IF we furvey the ten paftorals in a general view, it will be found that VIRGIL can derive from them very little claim to the praife of an inventor.   To fearch into the antiquity of this kind of poetry, is not my prefent purpofe; that it has long fubfifted in the eaft, the SACRED WRITINGS fufficiently inform us; and we may conjecture, with great probability, that it was fometimes the devotion, and fometimes the entertainment of the firft generations of mankind. THEOCRITUS united elegance with fimplicity; and taught his fhepherds to fing with fo much eafe and harmony, that his countrymen defpairing to excel, forbore to imitate him; and the Greeks, however vain or ambitious, left him in quiet poffeffion of the garlands which the woodnymphs had beftowed upon him.

VIRGIL, however, taking advantage of another language, ventured to copy or to rival the SICILIAN BARD: he has written with greater fplendor of diction, and elevation of fentiment: but as the magnificence of his performances was more, the fimplicity was lefs; and, perhaps, where he excells THEOCRITUS, he fometimes obtains his fuperiority by deviat-

ing

ing from the pastoral character, and performing what THEOCRITUS never attempted.

YET, though I would willingly pay to THEO-CRITUS the honour which is always due to an original author, I am far from intending to depreciate VIRGIL; of whom HORACE justly declares, that the rural muses have appropriated to him their elegance and sweetness, and who, as he copied THEOCRITUS in his design, has resembled him likewise in his success; for, if we except CALPHURNIUS, an obscure author of the lower ages, I know not that a single pastoral was written after him by any poet, till the re-vival of literature.

BUT though his general merit has been universally acknowledged, I am far from thinking all the productions of his rural Thalia equally excellent: there is, indeed, in all his pastorals a strain of versification which it is vain to seek in any other poet; but if we except the first and the tenth, they seem liable either wholly or in part to considerable objections.

THE second, though we should forget the great charge against it, which I am afraid can never be refuted, might, I think, have perished, without any diminution of the praise of its author; for I know not that it contains one affecting sentiment or pleasing description, or one

passage

paſſage that ſtrikes the imagination or awakens the paſſions.

THE third contains a conteſt between two ſhepherds, begun with a quarrel of which ſome particulars might well be ſpared, carried on with ſprightlineſs and elegance, and terminated at laſt in a reconciliation : but, ſurely, whether the invectives with which they attack each other be true or falſe, they are too much degraded from the dignity of paſtoral innocence ; and inſtead of rejoicing that they are both victorious, I ſhould not have grieved could they have been both defeated.

THE poem to POLLIO is, indeed, of another kind : it is filled with images at once ſplendid and pleaſing, and is elevated with grandeur of language worthy of the firſt of Roman poets ; but I am not able to reconcile myſelf to the diſproportion, between the performance and the occaſion that produced it : that the golden age ſhould return becauſe POLLIO had a ſon, appears ſo wild a fiction, that I am ready to ſuſpect the poet of having written, for ſome other purpoſe, what he took this opportunity of producing to the public.

THE fifth contains a celebration of Daphnis, which has ſtood to all ſucceeding ages as the model of paſtoral elegies. To deny praiſe to a performance which ſo many thouſands have
laboured

laboured to imitate, would be to judge with too
little deference for the opinion of mankind : yet
whoever ſhall read it with impartiality, will find
that moſt of the images are of the mythological
kind, and, therefore, eaſily invented ; and that
there are few ſentiments of rational praiſe or
natural lamentation.

In the Silenus he again riſes to the dignity of
philoſophic ſentiments and heroic poetry.   The
addreſs to VARUS is eminently beautiful : but
ſince the compliment paid to GALLUS fixes the
tranſaction to his own time, the fiction of Silenus
ſeems injudicious ; nor has any ſufficient reaſon
yet been found, to juſtify his choice of thoſe
fables that make the ſubject of the ſong.

THE ſeventh exhibits another conteſt of the
tuneful ſhepherds : and, ſurely, it is not without
ſome reproach to his inventive power, that of
ten paſtorals VIRGIL has written two upon the
ſame plan.   One of the ſhepherds now gains an
acknowledged victory, but without any apparent
ſuperiority ; and the reader, when he ſees the
prize adjudged, is not able to diſcover how it
was deſerved.

OF the eighth paſtoral, ſo little is properly the
work of VIRGIL, that he has no claim to other
praiſe or blame than that of a tranſlator.

OF the ninth, it is ſcarce poſſible to diſcover
the deſign or tendency : it is ſaid, I know not
upon

upon what authority, to have been compofed from fragments of other poems; and except a few lines in which the author touches upon his own misfortunes, there is nothing that feems appropriated to any time or place, or of which any other ufe can be difcovered than to fill up the poem.

THE firft and the tenth paftorals, whatever be determined of the reft, are fufficient to place their author above the reach of rivalry. The complaint of GALLUS difappointed in his love, is full of fuch fentiments as difappointed love naturally produces; his wifhes are wild, his re-fentment is tender, and his purpofes are incon-ftant. In the genuine language of defpair, he fooths himfelf a-while with the pity that fhall be paid him after his death:

> ———*Tamen cantabitis, Arcades, inquit,*
> *Montibus hæc veftris: foli cantare periti*
> *Arcades. O mihi tum quam molliter offa quiefcant,*
> *Veftra meos olim fi fiftula dicat amores!*

> ———Yet, O Arcadian fwains,
> Ye beft artificers of foothing ftrains!
> Tune your foft reeds, and teach your rocks
>     my woes,
> So fhall my fhade in fweeter reft repofe.
> O that your birth and bufinefs had been mine;
> To feed the flock, and prune the fpreading
>     vine!    WARTON.

DIS-

DISCONTENTED with his present condition, and desirous to be any thing but what he is, he wishes himself one of the shepherds. He then catches the idea of rural tranquillity; but soon discovers how much happier he should be in these happy regions, with LYCORIS at his side.

*Hic gelidi fontes, hic mollia prata, Lycori:*
*Hic nemus; hic ipso tecum consumerer ævo.*
*Nunc insanus amor duri me Martis in armis;*
*Tela inter media, atque adversis detinet hostes.*
*Tu procul a patria (nec sit mihi credere) tantum*
*Alpinas, ab dura, nives, & frigore Rheni*
*Me sine sola vides. Ah te ne frigora lædant!*
*Ah tibi ne teneras glacies secet aspera plantas!*

Here cooling fountains roll thro' flow'ry
   meads,
Here woods, Lycoris, lift their verdant heads;
Here could I wear my careless life away,
And in thy arms insensibly decay.
Instead of that, me frantic love detains
'Mid foes, and dreadful darts, and bloody
   plains:
While you—and can my soul the tale
   believe,
Far from your country, lonely wand'ring
   leave
Me, me your lover, barbarous fugitive!

Seek

Seek the rough Alps where ſnows eternal
    ſhine,
And joyleſs borders of the frozen Rhine.
Ah ! may no cold e'er blaſt my deareſt maid,
Nor pointed ice thy tender feet invade !

WARTON.

HE then turns his thoughts on every ſide, in
queſt of ſomething that may ſolace or amuſe
him : he propoſes happineſs to himſelf, firſt in
one ſcene and then in another ; and at laſt finds
that nothing will ſatisfy :

*Jam neque Hamadryades rurſum, nec carmina nobis*
*Ipſa placent : ipſæ rurſum conѣedite ſylvæ.*
*Non illum noſtri poſſunt mutare labores ;*
*Nec ſi frigoribus mediis Hebrumque bibamus,*
*Scithoniaſque nives hyemis ſubeamus aquoſæ :*
*Nec ſi, cum moriens alta liber aret in ulmo,*
*Æthiopum verſemus oves ſub ſidere Cancri,*
*Omnia vincit amor ; et nos cedamus amori.*

But now again no more the woodland maids,
Nor paſtoral ſongs delight—Farewell, ye
    ſhades—
No toils of ours the cruel god can change,
'Tho' loſt in frozen deſerts we ſhould range ;
Tho' we ſhould drink where chilling Hebrus
    flows,
Endure bleak winter's blaſts, and Thracian
    ſnows ;

Or

Or on hot India's plains our flocks should feed,
Where the parch'd elm declines his sickening
   head ;
Beneath fierce-glowing Cancer's fiery beams,
Far from cool breezes and refreshing streams.
Love over all maintains resistless sway,
And let us love's all-conquering power obey.
WARTON.

BUT notwithstanding the excellence of the
tenth pastoral, I cannot forbear to give the pre-
ference to the first, which is equally natural and
more diversified. The complaint of the shep-
herd, who saw his old companion at ease in the
shade, while himself was driving his little flock
he knew not whither, is such as, with variation
of circumstances, misery always utters at the
sight of prosperity :

*Nos patriæ fines, & dulcia linquimus arva ;*
*Nos patriam fugimus : tu, Tityre, lentus in umbra,*
*Formosam resonare doces Amaryllida sylvas.*

We leave our country's bounds, our much
   lov'd plains ;
We from our country fly, unhappy swains !
You, Tit'rus, in the groves at leisure laid,
Teach Amaryllis' name to every shade.
WARTON.

His account of the difficulties of his journey, gives a very tender image of pastoral distress:

> ————————*En ipse capellas*
> *Protenus æger ago : hanc etiam vix, Tityre, duco:*
> *Hic inter densas corylos modo namque gemellos,*
> *Spem gregis, ah! silice in nuda connixa reliquit.*

> And lo ! sad part'ner of the general care,
> Weary and faint I drive my goats afar !
> While scarcely this my leading hand sustains,
> Tir'd with the way, and recent from her pains ;
> For 'mid yon tangled hazels as we past,
> On the bare flints her hapless twin she cast,
> The hopes and promise of my ruin'd fold !
> WARTON.

The description of VIRGIL's happiness in his little farm, combines almost all the images of rural pleasure ; and he, therefore, that can read it with indifference, has no sense of pastoral poetry :

> *Fortunate senex, ergo tua rura manebunt,*
> *Et tibi magna satis ; quamvis lapis omnia nudus,*
> *Limosoque palus obducat pascua junco,*
> *Non insueta gravis tentabunt pabula fœtas,*
> *Nec mala vicini pecoris contagia lædent.*
> *Fortunate senex, his inter flumina nota,*

*Et*

*Et fontes facros, frigus captabis opacum.*
*Hinc tibi, quæ femper vicino ab limite fepes,*
*Hyblæis apibus florem depafta falicti,*
*Sæpe levi fomnum fuadebit inire fufurro.*
*Hinc altâ fub rupe canet frondator ad auras ;*
*Nec tamen interea raucæ, tua cura, palumbes,*
*Nec gemere aëria ceffabit turtur ab ulmo.*

Happy old man ! then ftill thy farms reftor'd,
Enough for thee, fhall blefs thy frugal board.
What tho' rough ftones the naked foil o'er-
    fpread,
Or mafhy bulrufh rear its wat'ry head,
No foreign food thy teeming ewes fhall fear,
No touch contagious fpread its influence here.
Happy old man ! here 'mid th' accuftom'd
    ftreams
And facred fprings, you'll fhun the fcorch-
    ing beams ;
While from yon willow-fence, thy pafture's
    bound,
The bees that fuck their flow'ry ftores around,
Shall fweetly mingle, with the whifpering
    boughs,
Their lulling murmurs, and invite repofe :
While from fteep rocks the pruner's fong is
    heard ;
Nor the foft-cooing dove, thy fav'rite bird,

VOL. III.        K        Mean

Mean while shall ceafe to breathe her melting
   ftrain,
Nor turtles from th' aerial elm to plain.
WARTON.

IT may be obferved, that thefe two poems
were produced by events that really happened;
and may, therefore, be of ufe to prove, that we
can always feel more than we can imagine, and
that the moft artful fiction muft give way to
truth,

   T

I am, SIR,

Your humble fervant,

.

DUBIUS.

NUMB. 93. TUESDAY, September 25, 1753.

*Irritat, mulcet, falfis terroribus implet*
*Ut* MAGUS; *& modo me Thebis, modo ponit*
*Athenis.* HOR.

'Tis he who gives my breaft a thoufand pains,
Can make me feel each paffion that he feigns;
Enrage, compofe, with more than magic art;
With pity, and with terror, tear my heart;
And fnatch me, o'er the earth, or thro' the air,
To Thebes, to Athens, when he will, and
where. POPE.

WRITERS of a mixed character, that
abound in tranfcendent beauties and in
grofs imperfections, are the moft proper and moft
pregnant fubjects for criticifm. The regularity
and correctnefs of a VIRGIL or HORACE, almoft
confine their commentators to perpetual panegyric, and afford them few opportunities of di-
verfifying their remarks by the detection of latent
blemifhes. For this reafon, I am inclined to
think, that a few obfervations on the writings of
SHAKESPEARE, will not be deemed ufelefs or
unentertaining, becaufe he exhibits more numerous examples of excellencies and faults, of every
kind, than are, perhaps, to be difcovered in
any other author. I fhall, therefore, from time

K 2 to

to time, examine his merit as a poet, without blind admiration, or wanton invective.

As SHAKESPEARE is fometimes blameable for the conduct of his fables, which have no unity; and fometimes for his diction, which is obfcure and turgid; fo his characteriftical excellencies may poffibly be reduced to thefe three general heads: " his lively creative imagination; his " ftrokes of nature and paffion; and his prefer- " vation of the confiftency of his characters." Thefe excellencies, particularly the laft, are of fo much importance in the drama, that they amply compenfate for his tranfgreffions againft the rules of TIME and PLACE, which being of a more mechanical nature, are often ftrictly ob- ferved by a genius of the loweft order; but to portray characters naturally, and to preferve them uniformly, requires fuch an intimate knowledge of the heart of man, and is fo rare a portion of felicity, as to have been enjoyed, perhaps, only by two writers, HOMER and SHAKESPEARE.

OF all the plays of SHAKESPEARE, the TEMPEST is the moft ftriking inftance of his creative power. He has there given the reins to his boundlefs imagination, and has carried the romantic, the wonderful, and the wild, to the moft pleafing extravagance. The fcene is a defo- late ifland; and the characters the moft new and fingular that can well be conceived: a

prince

prince who practises magic, an attendant spirit, a monster the son of a witch, and a young lady who had been brought to this solitude in her infancy, and had never beheld a man except her father.

As I have affirmed that SHAKESPEARE's chief excellence is the consistency of his characters, I will exemplify the truth of this remark, by pointing out some master-strokes of this nature in the drama before us.

THE poet artfully acquaints us that PROSPERO is a magician, by the very first words which his daughter MIRANDA speaks to him:

If by your art, my dearest father, you have
Put the wild waters in this roar, allay them:

which intimate that the tempest described in the preceding scene, was the effect of PROSPERO's power. The manner in which he was driven from his dukedom of Milan, and landed afterwards on this solitary island, accompanied only by his daughter, is immediately introduced in a short and natural narration.

THE officers of his attendant Spirit, ARIEL, are enumerated with amazing wildness of fancy, and yet with equal propriety: his employment is said to be,

———To tread the ooze
Of the falt deep;
To run upon the fharp wind of the north;
To do—bufinefs in the veins o' th' earth,
When it is bak'd with froft;
———to dive into the fire; to ride
On the curl'd clouds.

IN defcribing the place in which he has concealed the Neapolitan fhip, ARIEL exprefles
the fecrecy of its fituation by the following circumftance, which artfully glances at another of
his fervices;

———In the deep nook, where once
Thou call'ft me up at midnight, to fetch dew
From the ftill-vext Bermudas.

ARIEL, being one of thofe elves or fpirits,
" whofe paftime is to make midnight mufh-
" rooms, and who rejoice to liften to the folemn
" curfew;" by whofe affiftance PROSPERO has
bedimm'd the fun at noon-tide,

And 'twixt the green fea and the azur'd vault,
Set roaring war;

has a fet of ideas and images peculiar to his ftation and office; a beauty of the fame kind with
that which is fo juftly admired in the ADAM of
MILTON,

Milton, whose manners and sentiments are all Paradisaical. How delightfully and how suitably to his character, are the habitations and pastimes of this invisible being pointed out in the following exquisite song !

> Where the bee sucks, there suck I :
> In a cowslip's bell I lie ;
> There I couch when owls do cry.
> On the bat's back I do fly,
> After sun-set, merrily.
> Merrily merrily shall I live now,
> Under the blossom that hangs on the bough.

Mr. Pope, whose imagination has been thought by some the least of his excellencies, has, doubtless, conceived and carried on the machinery in his " Rape of the Lock," with vast exuberance of fancy. The images, customs, and employments of his Sylphs, are exactly adapted to their natures, are peculiar and appropriated, are all, if I may be allowed the expression, Sylphish. The enumeration of the punishments they were to undergo, if they neglected their charge, would, on account of its poetry and propriety, and especially the mixture of oblique satire, be superior to any circumstances in Shakespeare's Ariel, if we could suppose Pope to have been unacquainted with

K 4 the

the TEMPEST, when he wrote this part of his
accomplifhed poem.

———She did confine thee
Into a cloven pine ; within which rift
Imprifon'd, thou didft painfully remain
A dozen years : within which fpace fhe dy'd,
And left thee there ; where thou didft vent
   thy groans,
As faft as mill-wheels ftrike.

IF thou more murmur'ft, I will rend an oak,
And peg thee in his knotty entrails, 'till
Thou'ft howl'd away twelve winters.

FOR this, befure, to-night thou fhalt have
   cramps,
Side-ftitches that fhall pen thy breath up :
   urchins
Shall, for that vaft of night that they may work,
All exercife on thee ; thou fhalt be pinch'd
As thick as honey-combs, each pinch more
   ftinging
Than bees that made 'em.

IF thou neglect'ft or doft unwillingly
What I command, I'll rack thee with old
   cramps ;
Fill all thy bones with aches : make thee roar,
That beafts fhall tremble at thy din.
                    SHAKESPEARE.

WHATEVER spirit, careless of his charge,
Forsakes his post or leaves the Fair at large,
Shall feel sharp vengeance soon o'ertake his
    sins,
Be stopp'd in vials, or transfix'd with pins;
Or plung'd in lakes of bitter washes lie,  ·
Or wedg'd whole ages in a bodkin's eye:
Gums and pomatums shall his flight restrain,
While clog'd he beats his silken wings in vain;
Or allum styptics with contracting pow'r,
Shrink his thin essence like a shrivell'd flow'r:
Or as Ixion fix'd, the wretch shall feel
The giddy motion of the whirling wheel;
In fumes of burning chocolate shall glow,
And tremble at the sea that froths below!

                                    POPE.


THE method which is taken to induce FER-
DINAND to believe that his father was drown'd
in the late tempest, is exceedingly solemn and
striking.   He is sitting upon a solitary rock, and
weeping over-against the place where he imagined his father was wrecked, when he suddenly
hears with astonishment aërial music creep by
him upon the waters, and the SPIRIT gives him
the following information in words not proper
for any but a SPIRIT to utter:

Full fathom five thy father lies:
  Of his bones are coral made:

            K 5                       Those

Thofe are pearls that were his eyes:
   Nothing of him that doth fade,
But doth fuffer a fea-change,
Into fomething rich and ftrange.

And then follows a moft lively circumftance;

Sea-nymphs hourly ring his knell.
' Hark! now I hear them—Ding-dong-bell!

This is fo truly poetical, that one can fcarce forbear exclaiming with FERDINAND,

There is no mortal bufinefs, nor no found
That the earth owns!—

THE happy verfatility of SHAKESPEARE's genius enables him to excel in lyric as well as in dramatic poefy.

BUT the poet rifes ftill higher in his management of this character of ARIEL, by making a moral ufe of it, that is, I think, incomparable, and the greateft effort of his art. ARIEL informs PROSPERO, that he has fulfilled his orders, and punifhed his brother and companions fo feverely, that if he himfelf was now to behold their fufferings, he would greatly compaffionate them. To which PROSPERO anfwers,

—Doft thou think fo, Spirit?
ARIEL.  Mine would, Sir, were I human.

PROSPERO.   And mine shall.

He then takes occasion, with wonderful dexterity and humanity, to draw an argument from
the incorporeality of ARIEL, for the justice and
necessity of pity and forgiveness:

> Hast thou, which art but air, a touch, a feeling
> Of their afflictions; and shall not myself,
> One of their kind, that relish all as sharply,
> Passion'd as they, be kindlier mov'd than thou
>   art ?

THE poet is a more powerful magician than
his own PROSPERO: we are transported into
fairy land; we are rapt in a delicious dream,
from which it is misery to be disturbed; all
around is enchantment !

> ———The isle is full of noises,
> Sounds, and sweet airs, that give delight and
>   hurt not.
> Sometimes a thousand twanging instruments
> Will hum about mine ears, and sometimes
>   voices;
> That, if I then had wak'd after long sleep,
> Will make me sleep again: and then in
>   dreaming,
> The clouds, methought, would open and
>   shew riches

Ready to drop upon me :—when I wak'd,
I cry'd to dream again !
Z

❖-❖-❖-❖-❖-❖ ❖-❖-❖-❖-❖-❖-❖-❖-❖-❖-❖-❖-❖

NUMB. 94. SATURDAY, *September* 29, 1753.

*Monſtro quod ipſe tibi poſſis dare.* JUV.

———— What I ſhew,
Thyſelf may freely on thyſelf beſtow.
DRYDEN.

To the ADVENTURER.

SIR,

YOU have ſomewhat diſcouraged the hope
of idleneſs by ſhewing, that whoever compares the number of thoſe who have poſſeſſed
fortuitous advantages, and of thoſe who have
been diſappointed in their expectations, will
have little reaſon to regiſter himſelf in the lucky
catalogue.

BUT as we have ſeen thouſands ſubſcribe to a
raffle, of which one only could obtain the prize ;
ſo idleneſs will ſtill preſume to hope, if the advantages, however improbable, are admitted to
lie within the bounds of poſſibility. Let the
drone, therefore, be told, that if by the error
of fortune he obtains the ſtores of the bee, he
cannot

cannot enjoy the felicity; that the honey which is not gathered by induſtry, will be eaten without reliſh, if it is not waſted in riot; and that all who become poſſeſſed of the immediate object of their hope, without any efforts of their own, will be diſappointed of enjoyment.

No life can be happy, but that which is ſpent in the proſecution of ſome purpoſe to which our powers are equal, and which we, therefore, proſecute with ſucceſs: for this reaſon it is abſurd to dread buſineſs, upon pretence that it will leave few intervals to pleaſure.  Buſineſs is that by which induſtry purſues its purpoſe, and the purpoſe of induſtry is ſeldom diſappointed: he who endeavours to arrive at a certain point, which he perceives himſelf perpetually to approach, enjoys all the happineſs which nature has allotted to thoſe hours, that are not ſpent in the immediate gratification of appetites by which our own wants are indicated, or of affections by which we are prompted to ſupply the wants of others.  The end propoſed by the buſy, is various as their temper, conſtitution, habits, and circumſtances: but in the labour itſelf is the enjoyment, whether it be purſued to ſupply the neceſſaries or the conveniencies of life, whether to cultivate a farm or decorate a palace; for when the palace is decorated, and the barn filled, the pleaſure is at an end, till the object of deſire is

again

again placed at a diftance, and our powers are
again employed to obtain it with apparent fuccefs.
Nor is the value of life lefs, than if our enjoyment did not thus confift in anticipation ; for by
anticipation, the pleafure which would otherwife
be contracted within an hour, is diffufed through
a week ; and if the dread which exaggerates future evil is confeffed to be an increafe of mifery,
the hope which magnifies future good cannot be
denied to be an acceffion of happinefs.

THE moft numerous clafs of thofe who prefume to hope for miraculous advantages, is that
of gamefters.   But by gamefters, I do not mean
the gentlemen who ftake an eftate, againft the
cunning of thofe who have none ; for I leave the
cure of lunatics to the profeffors of phyfic : I
mean the diffolute and indigent, who in the common phrafe put themfelves in fortune's way, and
expect from her bounty that which they eagerly
defire, and yet believe to be too dearly purchafed
by diligence and induftry ; tradefmen who neglect their bufinefs, to fquander in fafhionable
follies more than it can produce ; and fwaggerers
who rank themfelves with gentlemen, merely
becaufe they have no bufinefs to purfue.

THE gamefter of this clafs will appear to be
equally wretched, whether his hope be fulfilled
or difappointed ; the object of it depends upon a
contingency, over which he has no influence ;
he

he purſues no purpoſe with gradual and percep-
tible ſucceſs, and, therefore, cannot enjoy the
pleaſure which ariſes from the anticipation of its
accompliſhment; his mind is perpetually on the
rack; he is anxious in proportion to the eager-
neſs of his deſire, and his inability to effect it;
to the pangs of ſuſpenſe, ſucceed thoſe of diſappointment; and a momentary gain only em-
bitters the loſs that follows.    Such is the life of
him, who ſhuns buſineſs becauſe he would ſecure leiſure for enjoyment; except it happens,
againſt the odds of a million to one, that a run
of ſucceſs puts him into the poſſeſſion of a ſum
ſufficient to ſubſiſt him in idleneſs the remainder
of his life: and in this caſe, the idleneſs which
made him wretched while he waited for the
bounty of fortune, will neceſſarily keep him
wretched after it is beſtowed: he will find,
that in the gratification of his appetites he can
fill but a ſmall portion of his time, and that
theſe appetites themſelves are weakened by
every attempt to increaſe the enjoyment which
they were intended to ſupply; he will, therefore, either doze away life in a kind of liſtleſs
indolence, which he deſpairs to exalt into felicity, or he will imagine that the good he wants
is to be obtained by an increaſe of his wealth,
by a larger houſe, a more ſplendid equipage,
and a more numerous retinue.    If with this
notion he has again recourſe to the altar of
fortune,

fortune, he will either be undeceived by a new series of fuccefs, or he will be reduced to his original indigence by the lofs of that which he knew not how to enjoy: if this happens, of which there is the higheft degree of probability, he will inftantly become more wretched in proportion as he was rich ; though, while he was rich, he was not more happy in proportion as he had been poor. Whatever is won, is reduced by experiment to its intrinfic value; whatever is loft, is heightened by imagination to more. Wealth is no fooner diffipated, than its inanity is forgotten, and it is regretted as the means of happinefs which it was not found to afford. The gamefter, therefore, of whatever clafs, plays againft manifeft odds ; fince that which he wins he difcovers to be brafs, and that which he lofes he values as gold. And it fhould alfo be remarked, that in this eftimate of his life, I have not fuppofed him to lofe a fingle ftake which he had not firft won.

But though gaming in general is wifely prohibited by the legiflature, as productive not only of private but of public evil ; yet there is one fpecies to which all are fometimes invited, which equally encourages the hope of idlenefs, and relaxes the vigour of induftry.

Ned Froth, who had been feveral years butler in a family of diftinction, having faved
                                        about

about four hundred pounds, took a little house
in the suburbs, and laid in a stock of liquors
for which he paid ready money, and which were,
therefore, the best of the kind. NED perceived
his trade increase; he pursued it with fresh alacrity,
he exulted in his success, and the joy of
his heart sparkled in his countenance: but it
happened that NED, in the midst of his happiness
and prosperity, was prevailed upon to buy a
lottery ticket. The moment his hope was fixed
upon an object which industry could not obtain,
he determined to be industrious no longer: to
draw drink for a dirty and boisterous rabble, was
a slavery to which he now submitted with reluctance,
and he longed for the moment in
which he should be free: instead of telling his
story, and cracking his joke for the entertainment
of his customers, he received them with
indifference, was observed to be silent and sullen,
and amused himself by going three or four times
a day to search the register of fortune for the
success of his ticket.

IN this disposition NED was sitting one morning
in the corner of a bench by his fire-side,
wholly abstracted in the contemplation of his
future fortune; indulging this moment the hope
of a mere possibility, and the next shuddering
with the dread of losing the felicity which his
fancy had combined with the possession of ten
thousand pounds. A man well dressed entered
haftily,

haſtily, and enquired for him of his gueſts, who
many times called him aloud by his name, and
curſt him for his deafneſs and ſtupidity, before
NED ſtarted up as from a dream, and aſked with
a fretful impatience what they wanted. An affected confidence of being well received, and an
air of forced jocularity in the ſtranger, gave NED
ſome offence; but the next moment he catched
him in his arms in a tranſport of joy, upon receiving his congratulation as proprietor of the
fortunate ticket, which had that morning been
drawn a prize of the firſt claſs.

IT was not, however, long before NED diſcovered that ten thouſand pounds did not bring
the felicity which he expected; a diſcovery
which generally produces the diſſipation of
ſudden affluence by prodigality. NED drank,
and whored, and hired fidlers, and bought fine
clothes; he bred riots at Vauxhall, treated
flatterers, and damned plays. But ſomething
was ſtill wanting; and he reſolved to ſtrike a
bold ſtroke, and attempt to double the remainder of his prize at play, that he might
live in a palace and keep an equipage: but in
the execution of this project, he loſt the whole
produce of his lottery ticket, except five hundred pounds in Bank notes, which when he
would have ſtaked he could not find. This
ſum was more than that which had eſtabliſhed
him in the trade he had left; and yet, with
the

the power of returning to a ftation that was once the utmoft of his ambition, and of renewing that purfuit which alone had made him happy, fuch was the pungency of his regret, that in the defpair of recovering the money which he knew had produced nothing but riot, difeafe, and vexation, he threw himfelf from the Bridge into the Thames.

I am, SIR,

Your humble fervant,

CAUTUS.

NUMB. 95. TUESDAY, *October* 2, 1753.

——*Dulcique animos novitate tenebs.* OVID.

And with fweet novelty your foul detain.

IT is often charged upon writers, that with all their pretenfions to genius and difcoveries, they do little more than copy one another; and that compofitions obtruded upon the world with the pomp of novelty, contain only tedious repetitions of common fentiments, or at beft exhibit a tranfpofition of known images, and give a new

appear-

appearance to truth only by fome flight difference of drefs and decoration.

THE allegation of refemblance between authors, is indifputably true; but the charge of plagiarifm, which is raifed upon it, is not to be allowed with equal readinefs. A coincidence of fentiment may eafily happen without any communication, fince there are many occafions in which all reafonable men will nearly think alike. Writers of all ages have had the fame fentiments, becaufe they have in all ages had the fame objects of fpeculation; the interefts and paffions, the virtues and vices of mankind, have been diverfified in different times, only by uneffential and cafual varieties; and we muft, therefore, expect in the works of all thofe who attempt to defcribe tnem, fuch a likenefs as we find in the pictures of the fame perfon drawn in, different periods, of his life.

IT is neceffary, therefore, that before an author be charged with plagiarifm, one of the moft reproachful, though, perhaps, not the moft atrocious of literary crimes, the fubject on which he treats fhould be carefully confidered. We do not wonder, that hiftorians, relating the fame facts, agree in their narration; or that authors, delivering the elements of fcience, advance the fame theorems, and lay down the fame definitions: yet it is not wholly without ufe to mankind,

kind, that books are multiplied, and that differ-ent authors lay out their labours on the same subject; for there will always be some reason why one should on particular occasions, or to particular persons, be preferable to another; some will be clear where others are obscure, some will please by their style and others by their method, some by their embellishments and others by their simplicity, some by closeness and others by diffusion.

THE same indulgence is to be shewn to the writers of morality: right and wrong are immu-table; and those, therefore, who teach us to distinguish them, if they all teach us right, must agree with one another. The relations of social life, and the duties resulting from them, must be the same at all times and in all nations: some petty differences may be, indeed, produced, by forms of government or arbitrary customs; but the general doctrine can receive no alteration.

YET it is not to be desired, that morality should be considered as interdicted to all future writers: men will always be tempted to deviate from their duty, and will, therefore, always want a monitor to recall them; and a new book often seizes the attention of the public, without any other claim than that it is new. There is likewise in composition, as in other things, a perpetual vicissitude of fashion; and

truth

truth is recommended at one time to regard, by appearances which at another would expofe it to neglect; the author, therefore, who has judgment to difcern the tafte of his contemporaries, and fkill to gratify it, will have always an opportunity to deferve well of mankind, by conveying inftruction to them in a grateful vehicle.

THERE are likewife many modes of compofition, by which a moralift may deferve the name of an original writer: he may familiarife his fyftem by dialogues after the manner of the ancients, or fubtilize it into a feries of fyllogiftic arguments: he may enforce his doctrine by ferioufnefs and folemnity, or enliven it by fprightlinefs and gaiety; he may deliver his fentiments in naked precepts, or illuftrate them by hiftorical examples; he may detain the ftudious by the artful concatenation of a continued difcourfe, or relieve the bufy by fhort ftrictures, and unconnected effays.

To excel in any of thefe forms of writing, will require a particular cultivation of the genius; whoever can attain to excellence, will be certain to engage a fet of readers, whom no other method would have equally allured; and he that communicates truth with fuccefs, muft be numbered among the firft benefactors to mankind.

THE

THE same observation may be extended like-wife to the passions : their influence is uniform, and their effects nearly the same in every human breast : a man loves and hates, desires and avoids, exactly like his neighbour; resentment and ambition, avarice and indolence, discover themselves by the same symptoms, in minds distant a thousand years frome one another.

NOTHING, therefore, can be more unjust, than to charge an author with plagiarism, merely because he assigns to every cause its natural effect; and makes his personages act, as others in like circumstances have always done. There are conceptions in which all men will agree, though each derives them from his own observation : whoever has been in love, will represent a lover impatient of every idea that interrupts his meditations on his mistress, retiring to shades and solitude, that he may amuse without disturbance on his approaching happiness, or associating himself with some friend that flatters his passion, and talking away the hours of absence upon his darling subject. Whoever has been so unhappy as to have felt the miseries of long-continued hatred, will, without any assistance from ancient volumes, be able to relate how the passions are kept in perpetual agitation, by the recollection of injury and meditations of revenge; how the blood

boils

boils at the name of the enemy, and life is worn away in contrivances of mifchief.

Every other paffion is alike fimple and limited, if it be confidered only with regard to the breaft which it inhabits ; the anatomy of the mind, as that of the body, muft perpetually exhibit the fame appearances ; and though by the continued induftry of fucceffive inquirers, new movements will be from time to time difcovered, they can affect only the minuter parts, and are commonly of more curiofity than importance.

It will now be natural to inquire, by what arts are the writers of the prefent and future ages to attract the notice and favour of mankind. They are to obferve the alterations which time is always making in the modes of life, that they may gratify every generation with a picture of themfelves. Thus love is uniform, but courtfhip is perpetually varying : the different arts of gallantry, which beauty has infpired, would of themfelves be fufficient to fill a volume ; fometimes balls and ferenades, fometimes tournaments and adventures have been employed to melt the hearts of ladies, who in another century have been fenfible of fcarce any other merit than that of riches, and liftened only to jointures and pin-money. Thus the ambitious man has at all times been eager of wealth and power ; but thefe hopes have been gratified in fome countries by fuppli-

cating

cating the people, and in others by flattering the
prince : honour in some states has been only the
reward of military atchievements, in others it
has been gained by noisy turbulence and popular
clamours.  Avarice has worn a different form,
as she actuated the usurer of Rome, and the
stock-jobber of England ; and idleness itself, how
little soever inclined to the trouble of invention,
has been forced from time to time to change its
amusements, and contrive different methods of
wearing out the day.

HERE then is the fund, from which those who
study mankind may fill their compositions with
an inexhaustible variety of images and allusions :
and he must be confessed to look with little attention upon scenes thus perpetually changing,
who cannot catch some of the figures before they
are made vulgar by reiterated descriptions.

IT has been discovered by Sir ISAAC NEW-
TON, that the distinct and primogenial colours
are only seven ; but every eye can witness,
that from various mixtures, in various propor-
tions, infinite diversifications of tints may be
produced.  In like manner, the passions of the
mind, which put the world in motion, and
produce all the bustle and eagerness of the busy
crowds that swarm upon the earth ; the passions,
from whence arise all the pleasures and pains
that we see and hear of, if we analyse the

mind of man, are very few; but thofe few agitated and combined, as external caufes fhall
happen to operate, and modified by prevailing
opinions and accidental caprices, make fuch
frequent alterations on the furface of life, that
the fhow, while we are bufied in delineating it,
vanifhes from the view, and a new fet of objects
fucceed, doomed to the fame fhortnefs of dura-
tion with the former : thus curiofity may always
find employment, and the bufy part of mankind
will furnifh the contemplative with the materials
of fpeculation to the end of time.

THE complaint, therefore, that all topics are
preoccupied, is nothing more than the murmur
of ignorance or idlenefs, by which fome difcou-
rage others and fome themfelves : the mutability
of mankind will always furnifh writers with new
images, and the luxuriance of fancy may always
embellifh them with new decorations.

T

NUMB. 96. SATURDAY, October 6, 1753.

———*Fortunatos nimium, sua si bena nerint.*

VIRG.

O happy, if ye knew your happy state!

DRYDEN.

IN proportion as the enjoyment and infelicity of life depend upon imagination, it is of importance that this power of the mind should be directed in its operations by reason; and, perhaps, imagination is more frequently busy when it can only imbitter disappointment and heighten calamity; and more frequently slumbers when it might increase the triumph of success, or animate insensibility to happiness, than is generally perceived.

An ecclesiastical living of considerable value became vacant, and EVANDER obtained a recommendation to the patron. His friend had too much modesty to speak with confidence of the success of an application supported chiefly by his interest, and EVANDER knew that others had solicited before him; as he was not, therefore, much elevated by hope, he believed he should not be greatly depressed by a disappointment. The gentleman to whom he was recommended, received him with great courtesy; but upon

L 2 reading

reading the letter, he changed countenance, and discovered indubitable tokens of vexation and regret; then taking EVANDER by the hand, " Sir," said he, " I think it scarce less a mis- " fortune to myself than you, that you was not " five minutes sooner in your application. The " gentleman whose recommendation you bring, " I wish more than any other to oblige ; but I " have just presented the living to the person, " whom you saw take his leave when you en- " tered the room."

THIS declaration was a stroke, which EVAN-DER had neither skill to elude, nor force to resist. The strength of his interest, though it was not known time enough to increase his hope, and his being too late only a few minutes, though he had reason to believe his application had been pre-cluded by as many days, were circumstances which imagination immediately improved to aggravate his disappointment : over these he mused perpetually with inexpressible anguish, he related them to every friend, and lamented them with the most passionate exclamations. And yet, what happened to EVANDER more than he ex-pected ? nothing that he possessed was diminished, nor was any possibility of advantage cut off : with respect to these and every other reality, he was in the same state, as if he had never heard of the vacancy, which he had some chance to

fill :

fill : but EVANDER groaned under the tyranny of imagination; and in a fit of caufelefs fretfulnefs caſt away peace, becaufe time was not ſtopped in its career, and a miracle did not interpofe to fecure him a living.

AGENOR, on whom the living which EVANDER folicited was beſtowed, never conceived a fingle doubt that he ſhould fail in his attempt : his character was unexceptionable, and his recommendation fuch as it was believed no other could counterbalance; he, therefore, received the bounty of his patron without much emotion; he regarded his fuccefs as an event produced, like rain and fun-ſhine, by the common and regular operation of natural caufes; and took poffeffion of his rectory with the fame temper, that he would have reaped a field he had fown, or received the intereſt of a fum which he had placed in the funds. But having, by accident, heard the report which had been circulated by the friends of EVANDER, he was at once ſtruck with a fenfe of his good fortune; and was fo affected by a retrofpect on his danger, that he could fcarce believe it to be paſt. "How providential," faid he, "was it, that I did not ſtay to drink another "difh of tea at breakfaſt, that I found a hackney- "coach at the end of the ſtreet, and that I met "with no ſtop by the way !" What an alteration was produced in AGENOR's conception of the

ad-

advantage of his fituation, and the means by
which it was obtained ! and yet at laft he had
gained nothing more than he expected; his
danger was not known time enough to alarm his
fear; the value of his acquifition was not increafed; nor had PROVIDENCE interpofed farther
than to exclude chance from the government of
the world. But AGENOR did not before reflect
that any gratitude was due to PROVIDENCE but
for a miracle; he did not enjoy his preferment
as a gift, nor eftimate his gain but by the probability of lofs.

As fuccefs and difappointment are under the
influence of imagination, fo are eafe and health;
each of which may be confidered as a kind of
negative good, that may either degenerate into
wearifomnefs and difcontent, or be improved
into complacency and enjoyment.

ABOUT three weeks ago I paid an afternoon
vifit to CURIO. CURIO is the proprietor of an
eftate which produces three thoufand pounds a
year, and the hufband of a lady remarkable for
her beauty and her wit; his age is that in which
manhood is faid to be compleat, his conftitution
is vigorous, his perfon graceful, and his underftanding ftrong. I found him in full health,
lolling in an eafy chair; his countenance was
florid, he was gayly dreffed, and furrounded with
all the means of happinefs which wealth well

ufed

used could bestow. After the first ceremonies had passed, he threw himself again back in his chair upon my having refused it, looked wistfully at his fingers ends, crossed his legs, enquired the news of the day, and in the midst of all possible advantages seemed to possess life with a listless indifference; which, if he could have preserved in contrary circumstances, would have invested him with the dignity of a stoic.

It happened that yesterday I paid Curio another visit. I found him in his chamber; his head was swathed in flannel, and his countenance was pale. I was alarmed at these appearances of disease, and enquired with an honest solicitude how he did. The moment he heard my question, he started from his seat, sprang towards me, caught me by the hand, and told me, in an exstasy, that he was in Heaven.

What difference in Curio's circumstances produced this difference in his sensations and behaviour? What prodigious advantage had now accrued to the man, who before had ease and health, youth, affluence, and beauty? Curio, during the ten days that preceded my last visit, had been tormented with the tooth-ach; and had, within the last hour, been restored to ease, by having the tooth drawn.

And is human reason so impotent, and imagination so perverse, that ease cannot be enjoyed

till

till it has been taken away? Is it not poſſible to improve negative into poſitive happineſs, by reflection? Can he, who poſſeſſes eaſe and health, whoſe food is taſteful, and whoſe ſleep is ſweet, remember, without exultation and delight, the ſeaſons in which he has pined in the languor of inappetence, and counted the watches of the night with reſtleſs anxiety?

Is an acquieſcence in the diſpenſations of UNERRING WISDOM, by which ſome advantage appears to be denied, without recalling trivial and accidental circumſtances that can only aggravate diſappointment, impoſſible to reaſonable beings? And is a ſenſe of the DIVINE BOUNTY neceſſarily languid, in proportion as that bounty appears to be leſs doubtful and interrupted?

EVERY man, ſurely, would bluſh to admit theſe ſuppoſitions; let every man, therefore, deny them by his life. He, who brings imagination under the dominion of reaſon, will be able to diminiſh the evil of life, and to increaſe the good; he will learn to reſign with complacency, to receive with gratitude, and poſſeſs with chearfulneſs: and as in this conduct there is not only wiſdom but virtue, he will under every calamity be able to rejoice in hope, and to anticipate the felicity of that ſtate, in which, " the SPIRITS " of the JUST ſhall be made PERFECT."

NUMB. 97.   TUESDAY, *October* 9, 1753.

Χρὴ δὲ καὶ ἐν τοῖς ἤθεσιν ὥσπερ καὶ ἐν τῇ τῶν πραγμάτων
συστάσει, ἀεὶ ζητεῖν, ἢ τὸ ἀναγκαῖον, ἢ τὸ εἰκός.

ARIST. POET.

As well in the conduct of the manners as in the constitution of the fable, we must always endeavour to produce either what is necessary or what is probable.

" WHOEVER ventures," says HORACE, " to form a character totally original, " let him endeavour to preserve it with uni-" formity and consistency ; but the formation of " an original character is a work of great dif-" ficulty and hazard."   In this arduous and uncommon task, however, SHAKESPEARE has wonderfully succeeded in his TEMPEST : the monster CALYBAN is the creature of his own imagination, in the formation of which he could derive no assistance from observation or experience.

. CALYBAN is the son of a witch, begotten by a demon : the sorceries of his mother were so terrible, that her countrymen banished her into this desart island as unfit for human society : in conformity, therefore, to this diabolical propagation, he is represented as a prodigy of cruelty,

L 5

malice,

malice, pride, ignorance, idleneſs, gluttony, and
luſt.    He is introduced with great propriety,
curſing Prospero and Miranda whom he had
endeavoured to defile; and his execrations are
artfully contrived to have reference to the occupation of his mother :

> As wicked dew, as e'er my mother bruſh'd
> With raven's feather from unwholeſome fen,
> Drop on you both !————————
> ————————All the charms
> Of Sycorax, toads, beetles, bats, light on you !

His kindneſs is, afterwards, expreſſed as much
in character, as his hatred, by an enumeration
of offices, that could be of value only in a deſolate iſland, and in the eſtimation of a ſavage :

> I pr'ythee, let me bring thee where crabs grow;
> And I with my long nails will dig the pig-
>     nuts ;
> Shew thee a jay's neſt ; and inſtruct thee how
> To ſnare the nimble marmazet.  I'll bring thee
> To cluſt'ring filberds ; and ſometimes I'll get
>     thee
> Young ſea-malls from the rock————
> I'll ſhew thee the beſt ſprings ; I'll pluck thee
>     berries ;
> I'll fiſh for thee, and get thee wood enough.
>                                     Which

Which laſt is, indeed, a circumſtance of great uſe in a place, where to be defended from the cold was neither eaſy nor uſual; and it has a farther peculiar beauty, becauſe the gathering wood was the occupation to which CALYBAN was ſubjected by PROSPERO, who, therefore, deemed it a ſervice of high importance.

THE groſs ignorance of this monſter is repreſented with delicate judgment; he knew not the names of the ſun and moon, which he calls the bigger light and the leſs; and he believes that Stephano was the man in the moon, whom his miſtreſs had often ſhewn him: and when PROSPERO reminds him that he firſt taught him to pronounce articulately, his anſwer is full of malevolence and rage:

> You taught me language; and my profit on't
> Is, I know how to curſe :————

the propereſt return for ſuch a fiend to make for ſuch a favour. The ſpirits whom he ſuppoſes to be employed by PROSPERO perpetually to torment him, and the many forms and different methods they take for this purpoſe, are deſcribed with the utmoſt livelineſs and force of fancy:

> Sometimes like apes, that moe and chatter
>    at me;
> And after bite me; then like hedge-hogs, which

Lie tumbling in my bare-foot way, and mount
Their pricks at my foot-fall: ſometimes am I
All wound with adders, who with cloven
   tongues
Do hiſs me into madneſs.

IT is ſcarcely poſſible for any ſpeech to be
more expreſſive of the manners and ſentiments,
than that in which our poet has painted the brutal
barbarity and unſeeling ſavageneſs of this ſon
of Sycorax, by making him enumerate, with a
kind of horrible delight, the various ways in
which it was poſſible for the drunken ſailors to
ſurprize and kill his maſter:

———There thou may'ſt brain him,
Having firſt ſeiz'd his books ; or with a log
Batter his ſkull ; or paunch him with a ſtake ;
Or cut his wezand with thy knife———

He adds, in alluſion to his own abominable attempt, " above all be ſure to ſecure the daughter;
" whoſe beauty, he tells them, is incomparable."
The charms of MIRANDA could not be more
exalted, than by extorting this teſtimony from
ſo inſenſible a monſter.

SHAKESPEARE ſeems to be the only poet who
poſſeſſes the power of uniting poetry with propriety of character ; of which I know not an in-
ſtance more ſtriking, than the image CALYBAN
                      makes

makes ufe of to exprefs filence, which is at once
highly poetical, and exactly fuited to the wild-
nefs of the fpeaker :

> Pray you tread foftly, that the blind mole
>    may not
> Hear a foot-fall.————

I ALWAYS lament that our author has not
preferved this fierce and implacable fpirit in
CALYBAN, to the end of the play; inftead of
which, he has, I think, injudicioufly put into
his mouth, words that imply repentance and
underftanding :

> ————I'll be wife hereafter
> And feek for grace.   What a thrice double afs
> Was I, to take this drunkard for a God,
> And worfhip this dull fool ?

IT muft not be forgotten, that SHAKESPEARE
has artfully taken occafion from this extraordinary character, which is finely contrafted to the
mildnefs and obedience of ARIEL, obliquely to
fatirize the prevailing paffion for new and wonderful fights, which has rendered the Englifh fo
ridiculous.   " Were I in England now," fays
TRINCULO, on firft difcovering CALYBAN,
" and had but this fifh painted, not an holiday
" fool there but would give a piece of filver.—
" When they will not give a doit to relieve a
" lame

" lame beggar, they will lay out ten to fee a
" dead Indian."

SUCH is the inexhauſtible plenty of our poet's
invention, that he has exhibited another character in this play, entirely his own ; that of the
lovely and innocent MIRANDA.

WHEN PROSPERO firſt gives her a fight of
prince FERDINAND, ſhe eagerly exclaims,

———What is't ? a ſpirit ?
Lord, how it looks about ! Believe me, Sir,
It carries a brave form.    But 'tis a ſpirit.

Her imagining that as he was ſo beautiful he muſt
neceſſarily be one of her father's aërial agents,
is a ſtroke of nature worthy admiration : as are
likewiſe her intreaties to her father not to uſe
him harſhly, by the power of his art ;

Why ſpeaks my father ſo ungently ?  This
Is the third man that e'er I ſaw ; the firſt
That e'er I ſigh'd for !———

Here we perceive the beginning of that paſſion,
which PROSPERO was deſirous ſhe ſhould feel for
the prince ; and which ſhe afterwards more fully
expreſſes upon an occaſion which diſplays at once
the tenderneſs, the innocence, and the ſimplicity of her character.  She diſcovers her lover
employed in the laborious taſk of carrying wood,
which

which PROSPERO had enjoined him to perform.
" Would," says she, " the lightning had burnt
" up those logs, that you are enjoined to pile !"

    ——If you'll fit down,
I'll bear your logs the while.  Pray give me that,
I'll carry't to the pile.——
——You look wearily.

It is by felecting fuch little and almoft impercep-
tible circumstances that SHAKESPEARE has more
truly painted the paffions than any other writer :
affection is more powerfully expreffed by this
fimple wish and offer of affiftance, than by the
unnatural eloquence and witticifms of DRYDEN,
or the amorous declamations of ROWE.

   THE refentment of PROSPERO for the match-
lefs cruelty and wicked ufurpation of his brother;
his parental affection and folicitude for the welfare of his daughter, the heirefs of his dukedom ;
and the awful folemnity of his character, as a
fkilful magician ; are all along preferved with
equal confiftency, dignity, and decorum.  One
part of his behaviour deferves to be particularly
pointed out : during the exhibition of a mafk
with which he had ordered ARIEL to entertain
FERDINAND and MIRANDA, he ftarts fuddenly
from the recollection of the confpiracy of CALY-
BAN and his confederates againft his life, and
difmiffes his attendant fpirits, who inftantly
                           vanifh

vanifh to a hollow and confufed noife. He appears to be greatly moved; and fuitably to this
agitation of mind, which his danger has excited,
he takes occafion, from the fudden difappearance
of the vifionary fcene, to moralize on the diffolution of all things :

————Thefe our actors
As I foretold you, were all fpirits : and
Are melted into air, into thin air.
And, like the bafelefs fabric of this vifion,
The cloud-capt towers, the gorgeous palaces,
The folemn temples, the great globe itfelf,
Yea, all which it inherit, fhall diffolve ;
And, like this unfubftantial pageant faded,
Leave not a rack behind————

To thefe noble images he adds a fhort but com-
prehenfive obfervation on human life, not excelled by any paffage of the moral and fententious EURIPIDES :

————We are fuch ftuff
As dreams are made on ; and our little life
Is rounded with a fleep !————

THUS admirably is an uniformity of character, that leading beauty in dramatic poefy,
preferved throughout the TEMPEST. And it
may be farther remarked, that the unities of
action, of place, and of time, are in this play,
though

though almost constantly violated by SHAKE-SPEARE, exactly observed.   The action is one, great, and entire, the restoration of PROSPERO to his dukedom; this business is transacted in the compass of a small island, and in or near the cave of PROSPERO; though, indeed, it had been more artful and regular to have confined it to this single spot; and the time which the action takes up, is only equal to that of the representation; an excellence which ought always to be aimed at in every well-conducted fable, and for the want of which a variety of the most entertaining incidents can scarcely atone.

Z

NUMB. 98.  SATURDAY, *October* 13, 1753.

*Aude aliquid brevibus Gyaris, et carcere dignum,*
*Si vis effe aliquis.*                    JUV.

Wou'dft thou to honours and preferments climb?
Be bold in mifchief, dare fome mighty crime,
Which dungeons, death or banifhment deferves.
                              DRYDEN.

To the ADVENTURER.

DEAR BROTHER, .

THE thirft of glory is I think allowed, even by the dull dogs who can fit ftill long enough to write books, to be a noble appetite.

MY ambition is to be thought a man of life and fpirit, who could conquer the world if he was to fet about it, but who has too much vivacity to give the neceffary attention to any fcheme of length.

I AM, in fhort, one of thofe heroic Adventurers, who have thought proper to diftinguifh themfelves by the titles of BUCK, BLOOD, and NERVE. When I am in the country, I am always on horfe-back, and I leap or break every hedge and gate that ftands in my way: when I am in town, I am conftantly to be feen at fome of the public places, at the proper times for
                                        making

making my appearance; as at Vaux-Hall, or
Marybone, about ten, very drunk: for though
I don't love wine, I am obliged to be con-
fumedly drunk five or fix nights in the week:
nay fometimes five or fix days together, for the
fake of my character.   Wherever I come, I
am fure to make all the confufion, and do all
the mifchief I can; not for the fake of doing
mifchief, but only out of frolick you know to
fhew my vivacity.   If there are women near
me, I fwear like a devil to fhew my courage,
and talk bawdy to fhew my wit.   Under the
rofe, I am a curfed favourite amongft them;
and have had " bonne fortune," let me tell
you.   I do love the little rogues hellifhly: but
faith I make love for the good of the public;
and the town is obliged to me for a dozen or
two of the fineft wenches that were ever brought
into its feraglios.   One, indeed, I loft: and,
poor fond foul! I pitied her! but it could not
be helped — felf-prefervation obliged me to
leave her—I could not tell her what was the
matter with her, rot me if I could; and fo it
got fuch a head, that the devil himfelf could
not have faved her.

THERE's one thing vexes me; I have much
ado to avoid having that infignificant character, a
good-natured fellow, fixed upon me; fo that I
am obliged in my own defence to break the boy's
head, and kick my whore down ftairs every time

I enter

I enter a night-houfe : I pick quarrels when I am not offended, break the windows of men I never faw, demolifh lamps, bilk hackney-coach-men, overturn wheelbarrows, and ftorm night-cellars : I beat the watchman, though he bids me good morrow, abufe the conftable, and in-fult the juftice : for thefe feats I am frequently kicked, beaten, pumped, profecuted, and im-prifoned ; but Tim is no flincher ; and if he does not get fame, blood ! he will deferve it.

I AM now writing at a coffee-houfe, where I am juft arrived, after a journey of fifty miles, which I have rode in four hours. I knocked up my blockhead's horfe two hours ago. The dog whipped and fpurred at fuch a rate, that I dare fay you may track him half the way by the blood ; but all would not do. The devil take the hindmoft, is always my way of travelling. The moment I difmounted, down dropt Dido, by Jove : and here am I all alive and merry, my old boy !

I'LL tell thee what ; I was a hellifh afs t'other day. I fhot a damn'd clean mare through the head, for jumping out of the road to avoid running over an old woman. But the bitch threw me, and I got a curfed flice on the cheek againft a flint, which put me in a paffion ; who could help it, you know ? Rot me ! I would not have loft her for five hundred old women, with all their brats, and the brats of
their

their brats to the third generation.—She was a sweet creature! I would have run her five-and-twenty miles within an hour, for five hundred pounds.   But she's gone!—Poor jade! I did love thee, that I did.

Now what you shall do for me old boy is this.  Help to raise my name a little, d'ye mind : write something in praise of us sprightly pretty fellows.  I assure you we take a great deal of pains for fame, and it is hard we should be bilkt. I would not trouble you, my dear; but only I fear I have not much time before me to do my own business ; for between you and I, both my constitution and estate are damnably out at elbows.   I intend to make them spin out together as evenly as possible ; but if my purse should happen to leak fastest, I propose to go with my last half-crown to Ranelagh gardens, and there, if you approve the scheme, I'll mount one of the upper alcoves, and repeat with an heroic air,

> " I'll boldly venture on the world unknown ;
> " It cannot use me worse than this has done."

I'll then shoot myself thro' the head; and so good by'tye.

Yours, as you serve me,

TIM. WILDGOOSE.

I SHOULD little deſerve the notice of a perſon ſo illuſtrious as the hero who honours me with the name of brother, if I ſhould caval at his principles or refuſe his requeſt. According to the moral philoſophy which is now in faſhion, and adopted by many of " the dull dogs who " write books," the gratification of appetite is virtue ; and appetite therefore, I ſhall allow to be noble, notwithſtanding the objections of thoſe who pretend, that whatever be its object, it can be good or ill in no other ſenſe than ſtature or complexion ; and that the voluntary effort only is moral by which appetite is directed or reſtrained, by which it is brought under the government of reaſon, and rendered ſubſervient to moral purpoſes.

BUT with whatever efforts of heroic virtue my correſpondent may have laboured to gratify his " thirſt of glory," I am afraid he will be diſappointed. It is, indeed, true, that like the heroes of antiquity, whom ſucceſſive generations have honoured with ſtatues and panegyric, he has ſpent his life in doing miſchief to others without procuring any real good to himſelf : but he has not done miſchief enough ; he has not ſacked a city or fired a temple ; he acts only againſt individuals in a contracted ſphere, and is loſt among a crowd of competitors, whoſe merit can only contribute to their mutual obſcurity, as the feats which are perpetually performed by innu-

merable

merable adventurers muſt ſoon become too common to conſer diſtinction.

In behalf of ſome among theſe candidates for
fame, the legiſlator has, indeed, thought fit to
interpoſe; and their atchievements are with great
ſolemnity· rehearſed and recorded in a temple,
of which I know not the celeſtial appellation,
but on earth it is called JUSTICE HALL in the
Old Bailey.

As the reſt are utterly neglected, I cannot
think of any expedient to gratify the noble thirſt
of my correſpondent and his compeers, but that
of procuring them admiſſion into this claſs ; an
attempt in which I do not deſpair of ſucceſs, for
I think I can demonſtrate their right, and I will
not ſuppoſe it poſſible that when this is done
they will be excluded.

Upon the moſt diligent examination of ancient hiſtory and modern panegyric, I find that
no action has ever been held honourable in ſo
high a degree, as killing men : this, indeed, is
one of the feats which our legiſlature has thought
fit to reſcue from oblivion, and reward in Jus-
TICE HALL : it has alſo removed an abſurd diſtinction, and, contrary to the practice of pagan antiquity, has comprehended the killers of
women, among thoſe who deſerve the rewards
that have been decreed to homicide.   Now he
may fairly be conſidered as a killer, who ſeduces

a young

a young beauty from the fondnefs of a parent, with whom fhe enjoys health and peace, the protection of the laws, and the fmile of fociety, to the tyranny of a bawd, and the exceffes of a brothel, to difeafe and diftraction, ftripes, infamy and imprifonment; calamities which cannot fail to render her days not only evil but few. It may, perhaps, be alleged, that the woman was not wholly paffive, but that in fome fenfe fhe may be confidered as felo de fe.    This, however, is mere cavil; for the fame may be faid of him who fights when he can run away; and yet it has always been deemed more honourable to kill the combatant than the fugitive.

IF this claim then of the BLOOD be admitted, and I do not fee how it can be fet afide, I propofe that after his remains fhall have been refcued from duft and worms, and confecrated in the temple of HYGEIA, called SURGEON's HALL, his bones fhall be purified by proper luftrations, and erected into a ftatue: that this ftatue fhall be placed in a niche, with the name of the hero of which it is at once the remains and the monument written over it, among many others of the fame rank, in the gallery of a fpacious building, to be erected by lottery for that purpofe: I propofe that this gallery be called the BLOOD's GALLERY; and, to prevent the labour and expence of emblazoning the atchievements of every individual, which

would

would be little more than repeating the same words, that an infcription be placed over the door to this effect : " This gallery is facred to " the memory and the remains of the BLOODS ; " heroes who lived in perpetual hoftility againft " themfelves and others ; who contracted dif- " eafes by excefs that precluded enjoyment, and " who continually perpetrated mifchief not in " anger but fport ; who purchafed this diftinc- " tion at the expence of life ; and whofe glory " would have been equal to ALEXANDER's, if " their power had not been lefs."

* * * * * * * * * * * * * * * * * * * * * * * * * * * * * * * *

NUMB. 99.   TUESDAY, *October* 16, 1753.

——*Magnis tamen excidit aufis.*      OVID.

·But in the glorious enterprize he dy'd.
                                          ADDISON.

IT has always been the practice of mankind, to judge of actions by the event. The fame attempts, conducted in the fame manner, but terminated by different fuccefs, produce different judgments : they who attain their wifhes, never want celebrators of their wifdom and their virtue ; and they that mifcarry, are quickly difcovered to have been defective not only in mental but in moral qualities. The world will never be long without some good reason to hate the unhappy: their real faults are immediately detected; and if those are not sufficient to sink them into infamy, an additional weight of calumny will be superadded: he that fails in his endeavours after wealth or power, will not long retain either honesty or courage.

THIS species of injustice has so long prevailed in universal practice, that it seems likewise to have infected speculation: so few minds are able to separate the ideas of greatness and prosperity, that even Sir WILLIAM TEMPLE has determined, " that he who can deserve the name of a hero, " must not only be virtuous but fortunate."

BY this unreasonable distribution of praise and blame, none have suffered oftner than PROJEC-TORS, whose rapidity of imagination and vastness of design raise such envy in their fellow mortals, that every eye watches for their fall, and every heart exults at their distresses: yet even a PRO-JECTOR may gain favour by success; and the tongue that was prepared to hiss, then endeavours to excel others in loudness of applause.

WHEN CORIOLANUS, in SHAKESPEARE, deserted to AUFIDIUS, the Volscian servants at first insulted him, even while he stood under the protection of the houshold Gods; but when they

saw

faw that the PROJECT took effect, and the
ftranger was feated at the head of the table, one
of them very judicioufly obferves, " that he
" always thought there was more in him than
" he could think."

MACHIAVEL has juftly animadverted on the
different notice taken by all fucceeding times, of
the two great projectors CATILINE and CÆSAR.
Both formed the fame PROJECT, and intended
to raife themfelves to power, by fubverting the
commonwealth : they purfued their defign, perhaps, with equal abilities, and with equal virtue ;
but CATILINE perifhed in the field, and CÆSAR
returned from Pharfalia with unlimited authority : and from that time, every monarch of the
earth has thought himfelf honoured by a com-
parifon with CÆSAR ; and CATILINE has been
never mentioned, but that his name might be
applied to traitors and incendiaries.

IN an age more remote, XERXES projected the
conqueft of Greece, and brought down the power
of Afia againft it : but after the world had been
filled with expectation and terror, bis army was
beaten, his fleet was deftroyed, and XERXES has
been never mentioned without contempt.

A FEW years afterwards, Greece likewife had
her turn of giving birth to a PROJECTOR ; who
invading Afia with a fmall army, went forward
in fearch of adventures, and by his efcape from

M 2　　　　　　　　　one

one danger, gained only more rashness to rush into another: he stormed city after city, over-ran kingdom after kingdom, fought battles only for barren victory, and invaded nations only that he might make his way through them to new invasions: but having been fortunate in the execution of his projects, he died with the name of ALEXANDER THE GREAT.

THESE are, indeed, events of ancient times; but human nature is always the same, and every age will afford us instances of public censures influenced by events. The great business of the middle centuries, was the holy war; which undoubtedly was a noble PROJECT, and was for a long time prosecuted with a spirit equal to that with which it had been contrived: but the ardour of the European heroes only hurried them to destruction; for a long time they could not gain the territories for which they fought, and, when at last gained, they could not keep them: their expeditions, therefore, have been the scoff of idleness and ignorance, their understanding and their virtue have been equally vilified, their conduct has been ridiculed, and their cause has been defamed.

WHEN COLUMBUS had engaged king Ferdinand in the discovery of the other hemisphere, the sailors, with whom he embarked in the expedition, had so little confidence in their comman-

der,

der, that after having been long at sea looking
for coasts which they expected never to find,
they raised a general mutiny, and demanded to
return. He found means to sooth them into a
permission to continue the same course three
days longer, and on the evening of the third
day descried land. Had the impatience of his
crew denied him a few hours of the time requested, what had been his fate but to have come
back with the infamy of a vain Projector,
who had betrayed the king's credulity to useless
expences, and risked his life in seeking countries that had no existence? how would those
that had rejected his proposals, have triumphed
in their acuteness? and when would his name
have been mentioned, but with the makers of
potable gold and malleable glass?

THE last royal Projectors with whom the
world has been troubled, were Charles of Sweden and the Czar of Muscovy. Charles, if
any judgment may be formed of his designs by
his measures and his enquiries, had purposed first
to dethrone the Czar, then to lead his army
through pathless desarts into China, thence to
make his way by the sword through the whole
circuit of Asia, and by the conquest of Turkey
to unite Sweden with his new dominions: but
this mighty Project was crushed at Pultowa;
and Charles has since been considered as a
madman by those powers, who sent their am-

bassadors

baffadors to folicit his friendfhip, and their ge-
nerals " to learn under him the art of war."

THE CZAR found employment fufficient in
his own dominions, and amufed himfelf in dig-
ging canals, and build ng cities; murdering his
fubjects with infufferable fatigues, and tranf-
planting nations from one corner of his dominions to another, without regretting the thou-
fands that perifhed on the way: but he attained
his end, he made his people formidable, and is
numbered by fame among the demi-gods.

I AM far from intending to vindicate the
fanguinary projects of heroes and conquerors,
and would wifh rather to diminifh the reputation
of their fuccefs, than the infamy of their mif-
carriages: for I cannot conceive, why he that
has burnt cities, wafted nations, and filled
the world with horror and defolation, fhould be
more kindly regarded by mankind, than he that
died in the rudiments of wickednefs; why he
that accomplifhed mifchief fhould be glorious,
and he that only endeavoured it fhould be criminal. I would wifh CÆSAR and CATILINE,
XERXES and ALEXANDER, CHARLES and
PETER, huddled together in obfcurity or deteftation.

BUT there is another fpecies of PROJECTORS,
to whom I would willingly conciliate mankind;
whofe ends are generally laudable, and whofe
labours are innocent; who are fearching out
new

new powers of nature, or contriving new works
of art; but who are yet perfecuted with inceffant
obloquy, and whom the univerfal contempt with
which they are treated, often debars from that
fuccefs which their induftry would obtain, if it
were permitted to act without oppofition.

THEY who find themfelves inclined to cenfure
new undertakings, only becaufe they are new,
fhould confider, that the folly of PROJECTION
is very feldom the folly of a fool; it is commonly the ebullition of a capacious mind, crouded with variety of knowledge, and heated with
intenfenefs of thought; it proceeds often from
the confcioufnefs of uncommon powers, from
the confidence of thofe, who having already
done much, are eafily perfuaded that they can do
more. When ROWLEY had compleated the
Orrery, he attempted the perpetual motion;
when BOYLE had exhaufted the fecrets of vulgar chemiftry, he turned his thoughts to the
work of tranfmutation.

A PROJECTOR generally unites thofe qualities
which have the faireft claim to veneration, extent
of knowledge, and greatnefs of defign: it was
faid of CATILINE, " immoderata, incredibilia,
" nimis alta femper cupiebat." Projectors of all
kinds agree in their intellects, though they differ
in their morals; they all fail by attempting
things beyond their power, by defpifing vulgar
attainments, and afpiring to performances, to

M 4                    which,

which, perhaps, nature has not proportioned the force of man: when they fail, therefore, they fail not by idleneſs or timidity, but by raſh adventure and fruitleſs diligence.

THAT the attempts of ſuch men will often miſcarry, we may reaſonably expect; yet from ſuch men, and ſuch only, are we to hope for the cultivation of thoſe parts of nature which lie yet waſte, and the invention of thoſe arts which are yet wanting to the felicity of life. If they are, therefore, univerſally diſcouraged, art and diſcovery can make no advances. Whatever is attempted without previous certainty of ſucceſs, may be conſidered as a PROJECT, and amongſt narrow minds may, therefore, expoſe its author to cenſure and contempt; and if the liberty of laughing be once indulged, every man will laugh at what he does not underſtand, every PROJECT will be conſidered as madneſs, and every great or new deſign will be cenſured as a PROJECT. Men, unaccuſtomed to reaſon and reſearches, think every enterprize impracticable, which is extended beyond common effects, or compriſes many intermediate operations. Many that preſume to laugh at PROJECTORS, would conſider a flight through the air in a winged chariot, and the movement of a mighty engine by the ſteam of water, as equally the dreams of mechanic lunacy; and would hear, with equal negligence, of the union of the Thames and

Severn

Severn by a canal, and the fcheme of Albu-
querque, the viceroy of the Indies, who in the
rage of hoftility had contrived to make Egypt
a barren defart, by turning the Nile into the
Red Sea.

THOSE who have attempted much, have
feldom failed to perform more than thofe who
never deviate from the common roads of action :
many valuable preparations of chemiftry are
fuppofed to have rifen from unfuccefsful enquiries after the grand elixir : it is, therefore,
juft to encourage thofe who endeavour to en-
large the power of art, fince they often fucceed
beyond expectation ; and when they fail, may
fometimes benefit the world even by their mif-
carriages.

T

NUMB. 100. SATURDAY, *October* 20, 1753.

*Nemo repentè fuit turpiſſimus.* ——    JUV.

No man e'er reach'd the heights of vice at
. firſt.    TATE.

To the ADVENTURER.

SIR,

THOUGH the characters of men have,
perhaps, been eſſentially the ſame in all
ages, yet their external appearance has changed
with other peculiarities of time and place, and
they have been diſtinguiſhed by different names,
as new modes of expreſſion have prevailed : a
periodical writer, therefore, who catches the
picture of evaneſcent life, and ſhews the deformity of follies which in a few years will be
ſo changed as not to be known, ſhould be careful to expreſs the character when he deſcribes the
appearance, and to connect it with the name by
which it then happens to be called.  You have
frequently uſed the terms BUCK and BLOOD, and
have given ſome account of the characters which
are thus denominated ; but you have not conſidered them as the laſt ſtages of a regular progreſſion, nor taken any notice of thoſe which
precede them.  Their dependance upon each
other is, indeed, ſo little known, that many
                                    ſuppoſe

suppose them to be distinct and collateral claſses,
formed by perſons of oppoſite intereſts, taſtes,
capacities, and diſpoſitions : the ſcale, however,
conſiſts of eight degrees; GREENHORN, JEMMY,
JESSAMY, SMART, HONEST FELLOW, JOYOUS
SPIRIT, BUCK, and BLOOD.  As I have myſelf
paſſed through the whole ſeries, I ſhall explain
each ſtation by a ſhort account of my life, remarking the periods when my character changed
its denomination, and the particular incidents
by which the change was produced.

My father was a wealthy farmer in Yorkſhire;
and when I was near eighteen years of age, he
brought me up to London, and put me apprentice
to a conſiderable ſhopkeeper in the city.   There
was an aukward modeſt ſimplicity in my manner,
and a reverence of religion and virtue in my converſation.   The novelty of the ſcene that was
now placed before me, in which there were innumerable objects that I never conceived to exiſt,
rendered me attentive and credulous; peculiarities, which, without a provincial accent, a ſlouch
in my gait, a long lank head of hair, an unfaſhi-
onable ſuit of drab-coloured cloth, would have
denominated me a GREENHORN, or, in other
words, a country put very green.

GREEN, then, I continued even in externals,
near two years; and in this ſtate I was the object
of univerſal contempt and deriſion : but being at

M 6                        length

length wearied with merriment and infult, I was
very fedulous to affume the manners and appearance of thofe, who in the fame ftation were
better treated.  I had already improved greatly
in my fpeech ; and my father having allowed
me thirty pounds a year for apparel and pocket-
money, the greater part of which I had faved,
I befpoke a fuit of clothes of an eminent city
taylor, with feveral waiftcoats and breeches, and
two frocks for a change : I cut off my hair, and
procured a brown bob periwig of WILDING, of
the fame colour, with a fingle row of curls juft
round the bottom, which I wore very nicely
combed, and without powder : my hat, which
had been cocked with great exactnefs in an equi-
lateral triangle, I difcarded, and purchafed one
of a more fafhionable fize, the fore corner of
which projected near two inches further than
thofe on each fide, and was moulded into the
fhape of a fpout : I alfo furnifhed myfelf with a
change of white thread ftockings, took care that
my pumps were varnifhed every morning with
the new German blacking-ball ; and when I
went out, carried in my hand a little fwitch,
which, as it has been long appendent to the
character that I had juft affumed, has taken the
fame name, and is called a JEMMY.

I SOON perceived the advantage of this tranf-
formation.  My manner had not, indeed, kept

pace

pace with my drefs; I was ftill modeft and dif-
fident, temperate and fober, and confequently
ftill fubject to ridicule: but I was now admitted into company, from which I had before
been excluded by the rufticity of my appearance; I was rallied and encouraged by turns;
and I was inftructed both by precept and example. Some offers were made of carrying
me to a houfe of private entertainment, which
then I abfolutely refufed; but I foon found the
way into the play-houfe, to fee the two laft
acts and the farce: here I learned, that by
breaches of chaftity no man was thought to incur either guilt or fhame; but that, on the contrary, they were effentially neceffary to the character of a fine gentleman. I foon copied the
original, which I found to be univerfally admired, in my morals, and made fome farther ap-
proaches to it in my drefs: I fuffered my hair to
grow long enough to comb back over the fore-
top of my wig, which, when I fallied forth to
my evening amufement, I changed to a queue;
I tied the collar of my fhirt with half an ell of
black ribbon, which appeared under my neck-
cloth; the fore corner of my hat was confider-
ably elevated and fhortened, fo that it no longer
refembled a fpout, but the corner of a minced
pye; my waiftcoat was edged with a narrow
lace, my ftockings were filk, and I never appeared without a pair of clean gloves. My
address,

addrefs, from its native mafculine plainnefs, was converted to an excefs of foftnefs and civility, efpecially when I fpoke to the ladies. I had before made fome progrefs in learning to fwear; I had proceeded by fegs, faith, pox, plague, 'pon my life, 'pon my foul, rat it, and zookers, to zauns and the divill. Now I advanced to by Jove, 'fore ged, geds curfe it, and demme: but I ftill uttered thefe interjections in a tremulous tone, and my pronunciation was feminine and vicious. I was fenfible of my defects, and, therefore, applied with great diligence to remove them. I frequently practifed alone, but it was a long time before I could fwear fo much to my own fatisfaction in company, as by myfelf. My labour, however, was not without its reward; it recommended me to the notice of the ladies, and procured me the gentle appellation of JESSAMY.

I NOW learned among other GROWN GENTLEMEN to dance, which greatly enlarged my acquaintance; I entered into a fubfcription for country dances once a week at a tavern, where each gentleman engaged to bring a partner: at the fame time I made confiderable advances in fwearing; I could pronounce damme with a tolerable air and accent, give the vowel its full found, and look with confidence in the face of the perfon to whom I fpoke. About this time my father's elder brother

ther

ther died, and left me an estate of near five hundred pounds per annum. I now bought out the remainder of my time; and this sudden accession of wealth and independence gave me immediately an air of greater confidence and freedom. I laid out near one hundred and fifty pounds in clothes, though I was obliged to go into mourning: I employed a court taylor to make them up; I exchanged my queue for a bag; I put on a sword, which, in appearance at least, was a Toledo; and in proportion as I knew my dress to be elegant, I was less solicitous to be neat. My acquaintance now increased every hour; I was attended, flattered, and careffed; was often invited to entertainments, supped every night at a tavern, and went home in a chair; was taken notice of in public places, and was universally confessed to be improved into a SMART.

THERE were some intervals in which I found it necessary to abstain from wenching; and in these, at whatever risque, I applied myself to the bottle: a habit of drinking came insensibly upon me, and I was soon able to walk home with a bottle and a pint. I had learned a sufficient number of fashionable toasts, and got by heart several toping and several bawdy songs, some of which I ventured to roar out with a friend hanging on my arm as we scoured the street after our nocturnal revel. I now laboured

boured with indefatigable induſtry to increaſe
theſe acquiſitions : I enlarged my ſtock of
healths ; made great progreſs in ſinging, joking,
and ſtory telling ; ſwore well ; could make a
company of ſtaunch topers drunk ; always
collected the reckoning, and was the laſt man
that departed.   My face began to be covered
with red pimples, and my eyes to be weak ; I
became daily more negligent of my dreſs, and
more blunt in my manner ; I profeſſed myſelf a
foe to ſtarters and milkſops, declared that there
was no enjoyment equal to that of a bottle and
a friend, and ſoon gained the appellation of an
HONEST FELLOW.

By this diſtinction I was animated to attempt yet greater excellence ; I learned ſeveral
feats of mimickry of the under players, could
take off known characters, tell a ſtaring ſtory,
and humbug with ſo much ſkill as ſometimes
to take-in a knowing one.   I was ſo ſucceſsful
in the practice of theſe arts, to which, indeed,
I applied myſelf with unwearied diligence and
affiduity, that I kept my company roaring with
applauſe, till their voices ſunk by degrees, and
they were no longer able to laugh, becauſe they
were no longer able either to hear or to ſee.   I had
now aſcended another ſcale in the climax ; and
was acknowledged by all who knew me, to be a
JOYOUS SPIRIT.

AFTER

AFTER all thefe topics of merriment were exhaufted, and I had repeated my tricks, my ftories, my jokes, and my fongs, till they grew infipid, I became mifchievous; and was continually devifing and executing FROLICS, to the unfpeakable delight of my companions, and the injury of others. For many of them I was profecuted, and frequently obliged to pay large damages: but I bore all thefe loffes with an air of jovial indifference, I pufhed on in my career, I was more defperate in proportion as I had lefs to lofe; and being deterred from no mifchief by the dread of its confequences, I was faid to run at all, and, complimented with the name of BUCK.

MY eftate was at length mortgaged for more than it was worth; my creditors were importunate; I became negligent of myfelf and of others; I made a defperate effort at the gaming table, and loft the laft fum that I could raife; my eftate was feized by the mortgagee; I learned to pack cards and to cog a die; became a bully to whores; paffed my nights in a brothel, the ftreet, or the watch-houfe; was utterly infenfible of fhame, and lived upon the town as a beaft of prey in a foreft. Thus I reached the fummit of modern glory, and had juft acquired the diftinction of a BLOOD, when I was arrefted for an old debt of three hundred pounds, and thrown into the King's Bench prifon.

THESE

THESE characters, Sir, though they are diſtinct, yet do not all differ, otherwiſe than as ſhades of the ſame colour. And though they are ſtages of a regular progreſſion, yet the whole progreſs is not made by every individual : ſome are ſo ſoon initiated in the myſteries of the town, that they are never publickly known in their GREENHORN ſtate ; others fix long in their JEMMYHOOD, others are JESSAMIES at four-ſcore, and ſome ſtagnate in each of the higher ſtages for life. But I requeſt that they may never hereafter be confounded either by you or your correſpondents. Of the BLOOD, your brother Adventurer, Mr. WILDGOOSE, though he aſ-ſumes the character, does not ſeem to have a juſt and preciſe idea as diſtinct from the BUCK, in which claſs he ſhould be placed, and will pro-bably die ; for he ſeems determined to ſhoot him-ſelf, juſt at the time when his circumſtances will enable him to aſſume the higher diſtinction.

BUT the retroſpect upon life, which this let-ter has made neceſſary, covers me with confu-ſion, and aggravates deſpair. I cannot but re-flect, that among all theſe characters, I have never aſſumed that of a MAN. Man is a REA-SONABLE BEING, which he ceaſes to be, who diſguiſes his body with ridiculous fopperies, or degrades his mind by deteſtable brutality. Theſe thoughts would have been of great uſe to me, if they

they had occurred feven years ago.   If they are
of ufe to you, I hope you will fend me a fmall
gratuity for my labour, to alleviate the mifery of
hunger and nakednefs : but, dear Sir, let your
bounty be fpeedy, left I perifh before it arrives.

> I am your humble fervant,

Common fide, King's Bench,           NOMENTANUS.
> Oct. 18, 1753.

\*\*\*\*\*\*\*\*\*\*\*\*\*\*\*\*\*\*\*\*\*\*\*\*\*\*\*\*

NUMB. 101.   TUESDAY, *October* 23, 1753.

———————*Eſt ubi peccat.*           HOR.
———————Yet fometimes he miftakes.

### To the ADVENTURER.

SIR,

IF we confider the high rank which MILTON
has defervedly obtained among our few
Englifh claffics, we cannot wonder at the multitude of commentaries and criticifms of which
he has been the fubject.   To thefe I have added
fome mifcellaneous remarks : and if you fhould
at firft be inclined to reject them as trifling, you
may, perhaps, determine to admit them, when
you reflect that they are new.

THE defcription of Eden in the fourth book
of the PARADISE LOST, and the battle of the
> angels

angels in the fixth, are ufually felected as the
moft ftriking examples of a florid and vigorous
imagination : but it requires much greater
ftrength of mind to form an affemblage of natural objects, and range them with propriety and
beauty, than to bring together the greateft variety of the moft fplendid images, without any
regard to their ufe or congruity ; as in painting,
he who, by the force of his imagination, can de-
lineate a landfcape, is deemed a greater mafter
than he, who, by heaping rocks of coral upon
teffelated pavements, can only make abfurdity
fplendid, and difpofe gaudy colours fo as beft to
fet off each other.

" SAPPHIRE fountains that rolling over
" orient PEARL run NECTAR, rofes without
" thorns, trees that bear fruit of VEGETABLE
" GOLD, and that weep odorous gums and
" balms," are eafily feigned; but having no
relative beauty as pictures of nature, nor any
abfolute excellence as derived from truth, they
can only pleafe thofe, who, when they read, exercife no faculty but fancy, and admire becaufe
they do not think.

IF I fhall not be thought to digrefs wholly
from my fubject, I would illuftrate this remark,
by comparing two paffages, written by MILTON
and FLETCHER, on nearly the fame fubject.
The fpirit in COMUS thus pays his addrefs of
thanks to the water-nymph Sabrina :

May

> May thy brimmed waves for this,
> Their full tribute never miss,
> From a thousand petty rills,
> That tumble down the snowy hills:
> Summer drought, or singed air,
> Never scorch thy tresses fair;
> Nor wet October's torrent flood
> Thy molten chrystal fill with mud:

Thus far the wishes are most proper for the welfare of a river goddess: the circumstance of summer not scorching her tresses, is highly poetical and elegant: but what follows, though it is pompous and majestic, is unnatural and far fetched;

> May thy billows roll ashore
> The beryl and the golden ore:
> May thy lofty head be crown'd
> With many a tow'r and terras round;
> And here and there, thy banks upon,
> With groves of myrrh and cinnamon!

The circumstance in the third and fourth lines is happily fancied; but what idea can the reader have of an ENGLISH RIVER rolling GOLD and the BERYL ashore, or of groves of CINNAMON growing on its banks?  The images in the following passage of FLETCHER are all simple and real, all appropriated and strictly natural:

For

For thy kindnefs to me fhown,
Never from thy banks be blown
Any tree, with windy force,
Crofs thy ftream to ftop thy courfe;
May no beaft that comes to drink,
With his horns caft down thy brink;
May none that for thy fifh do look,
Cut thy banks to dam thy brook;
Barefoot may no neighbour wade
In thy cool ftreams, wife or maid,
When the fpawn on ftones do lie,
To wafh their hemp, and fpoil the fry.

THE glaring picture of Paradife is not, in my opinion, fo ftrong an evidence of MILTON's force of imagination, as his reprefentation of ADAM and EVE when they left it, and of the paffions with which they were agitated on that event.

AGAINST his battle of the Angels, I have the fame objections as againft his garden of Eden. He has endeavoured to elevate his combatants, by giving them the enormous ftature of giants in romances, books of which he was known to be fond; and the prowefs and behaviour of MICHAEL as much refemble the feats of ARIOSTO's Knight, as his two-handed fword does the weapons of chivalry: I think the fublimity of his genius much more vifible in the

firft

first appearance of the fallen Angels; the debates of the infernal peers; the paffage of Satan through the dominions of Chaos, and his adventure with Sin and Death; the miffion of RAPHAEL to ADAM; the converfations between ADAM and his wife; the creation; the account which ADAM gives of his firft fenfations, and of the approach of EVE from the hand of her CREATOR; the whole behaviour of ADAM and EVE after the firft tranfgreffion; and the profpect of the various flates of the world, and hiftory of man exhibited in a vifion to ADAM.

IN this vifion, MILTON judicioufly reprefents ADAM, as ignorant of what difafter had be- fallen ABEL, when he was murdered by his brother: but during his converfation with RA- PHAEL, the poet feems to have forgotten this neceffary and natural ignorance of the firft man. How was it poffible for ADAM to difcern what the ANGEL meant by " cubic phalanxes, by " planets of afpect malign, by encamping on " the foughten field, by van and rear, by ftand- " ards and gonfalons and glittering tiffues, by " the girding fword, by embattled fquadrons, " chariots, and flaming arms, and fiery fteeds?" And although ADAM poffeffed a fuperior degree of knowledge, yet doubtlefs he had not fkill enough in chemiftry to underftand RAPHAEL, who informed him, that

—Sulphurous

———————Sulphurous and nitrous foam
They found, they mingled, and with fubtle art,
CONCOCTED and ADUSTED, they reduc'd
To blackeft grain, and into ftore convey'd.

And, furely, the nature of cannon was not
much explained to ADAM, who neither knew
or wanted the ufe of iron tools, by telling him,
that they refembled the hollow bodies of oak
or fir,

> With branches lopt, in wood or mountain
> fell'd.      .

He that never beheld the brute creation but in
its paftimes and fports, muft have greatly wondered, when the ANGEL expreffed the flight of
the Satanic hoft, by faying, that they fled

> ———————— As a herd
> Of goats, or TIMOROUS flock, together
> throng'd.

BUT as there are many exuberances in this
poem, there appears to be alfo fome defects. As
the ferpent was the inftrument of the temptation,
MILTON minutely defcribes its beauty and al-
lurements : and I have frequently wondered, that
he did not, for the fame reafon, give a more
elaborate defcription of the tree of life ; efpé-
cially

cially as he was remarkable for his knowledge and imitation of the SACRED WRITINGS, and as the following paſſage in the REVELATIONS afforded him a hint, from which his creative fancy might have worked up a ſtriking picture: " In the midſt of the ſtreet of it, and of either " ſide of the river, was there the tree of life; which " bare twelve manner of fruits, and yielded her " fruit every month ; and the leaves of the tree " were for the healing of the nations."

AT the end of the fourth book, ſuſpenſe and attention are excited to the utmoſt; a combat between Satan and the guardians of Eden is eagerly expected, and curioſity is impatient for the action and the cataſtrophe : but this horrid fray is prevented, expectation is cut off, and curioſity diſappointed, by an expedient which, though applauded by ADDISON and POPE, and imitated from HOMER and VIRGIL, will be deemed frigid and inartificial, by all who judge from their own ſenſations, and are not content to echo the deciſions of others. The golden balances are held forth, " which," ſays the poet, " are yet ſeen between Aſtrea and the Scorpion;" Satan looks up, and perceiving that his ſcale mounted aloft, departs with the ſhades of night. To make ſuch a uſe, at ſo critical a time, of LIBRA, a mere imaginary ſign of the Zodiac, is ſcarcely juſtifiable in a poem founded on religious truth.

AMONG innumerable beauties in the PARA-
DISE LOST, I think the moſt tranſcendant is the
ſpeech of Satan at the beginning of the ninth
book : in which his unextinguiſhable pride and
fierce indignation againſt GOD, and his envy
towards MAN, are ſo blended with an involun-
tary approbation of goodneſs, and diſdain of the
meanneſs and baſeneſs of his preſent undertaking,
as to render it, on account of the propriety of its
ſentiments and its turns of paſſion, the moſt
natural, moſt ſpirited, and truly dramatic ſpeech,
that is, perhaps, to be found in any writer whether antient or modern : and yet Mr. ADDISON
has paſſed it over, unpraiſed and unnoticed.

IF an apology ſhould be deemed neceſſary for
the freedom here uſed with our inimitable bard,
let me conclude in the words of LONGINUS :
" Whoever was carefully to collect the ble-
" miſhes of HOMER, DEMOSTHENES, PLATO,
" and of other celebrated writers of the ſame
" rank, would find they bore not the leaſt pro-
" portion to the ſublimities and excellencies
" with which their works abound."

          Z          I am, SIR,

                         Your humble ſervant,

                                   PALÆOPHILUS.

NUMB. 102. SATURDAY, *October* 27, 1753.

*——Quid tam dextro pede concipis, ut te*
*Conatus non pæniteat utique peracti?*   JUV.

What in the conduct of our life appears
So well defign'd, fo luckily begun,
But, when we have our wifh, we wifh undone.
DRYDEN.

### To the ADVENTURER.

SIR,

I HAVE been for many years a trader in London.  My beginning was narrow, and my
ftock fmall; I was, therefore, a long time brow-
beaten and defpifed by thofe, who having more
money thought they had more merit than myfelf.
I did not, however, fuffer my refentment to in-
ftigate me to any mean arts of fupplantation, nor
my eagernefs of riches to betray me to any indi-
rect methods of gain; I perfued my bufinefs with
inceffant affiduity, fupported by the hope of
being one day richer than thofe who contemned
me; and had, upon every annual review of my
books, the fatisfaction of finding my fortune
increafed beyond my expectation.

IN a few years my induftry and probity were
fully recompenfed, my wealth was really great,

N 2                             and

and my reputation for wealth ſtill greater. I had large warehouſes crouded with goods, and conſiderable ſums in the public funds; I was careſſed upon the Exchange by the moſt eminent merchants; became the oracle of the common council; was ſolicited to engage in all commercial undertakings; was flattered with the hopes of becoming in a ſhort time one of the directors of a wealthy company; and, to complete my mercantile honours, enjoyed the expenſive happineſs of fining for ſheriff.

RICHES, you know, eaſily produce riches: when I had arrived to this degree of wealth, I had no longer any obſtruction or oppoſition to fear; new acquiſitions were hourly brought within my reach, and I continued for ſome years longer to heap thouſands upon thouſands.

AT laſt I reſolved to complete the circle of a citizen's proſperity by the purchaſe of an eſtate in the country, and to cloſe my life in retirement. From the hour that this deſign entered my imagination, I found the fatigues of my employment every day more oppreſſive, and perſuaded myſelf that I was no longer equal to perpetual attention, and that my health would ſoon be deſtroyed by the torment and diſtraction of extenſive buſineſs. I could image to myſelf no happineſs, but in vacant jollity, and uninterrupted leiſure; nor entertain my friends with any other topic, than

the

the vexation and uncertainty of trade, and the happiness of rural privacy.

BUT notwithstanding these declarations, I could not at once reconcile myself to the thoughts of ceasing to get money ; and though I was every day enquiring for a purchase, I found some reason for rejecting all that were offered me ; and, indeed, had accumulated so many beauties and conveniences in my idea of the spot, where I was finally to be happy, that, perhaps, the world might have been travelled over, without discovery of a place which would not have been defective in some particular.

THUS I went on still talking of retirement, and still refusing to retire ; my friends began to laugh at my delays, and I grew ashamed to trifle longer with my own inclinations ; an estate was at length purchased, I transferred my stock to a prudent young man who had married my daughter, went down into the country, and commenced lord of a spacious manor.

HERE for some time I found happiness equal to my expectation. I reformed the old house according to the advice of the best architects, I threw down the walls of the garden, and inclosed it with pallisades, planted long avenues of trees, filled a green-house with exotic plants, dug a new canal, and threw the earth into the old moat.

THE

THE fame of thefe expenfive improvements brought in all the country to fee the fhew. I entertained my vifiters with great liberality, led them round my gardens, fhewed them my apartments, laid before them plans for new decorations, and was gratified by the wonder of fome and the envy of others.

I WAS envied ; but how little can one man judge of the condition of another ? The time was now coming, in which affluence and fplendor could no longer make me pleafed with myfelf. I had built till the imagination of the architect was exhaufted ; I had added one convenience to another, till I knew not what more to wifh or to defign ; I had laid out my gardens, planted my park, and compleated my waterworks ; and what now remained to be done ? what, but to look up to turrets, of which when they were once raifed I had no farther ufe, to range over apartments where time was tarnifhing the furniture, to ftand by the cafcade of which I fcarcely now perceived the found, and to watch the growth of woods that muft give their fhade to a diftant generation.

IN this gloomy inactivity, is every day begun and ended : the happinefs that I have been fo long procuring is now at an end, becaufe it has been procured ; I wander from room to room till I am weary of myfelf ; I ride out to a neighbouring

bouring hill in the centre of my estate, from whence all my lands lie in prospect round me; I see nothing that I have not seen before, and return home disappointed, though I knew that I had nothing to expect.

In my happy days of business I had been accustomed to rise early in the morning; and remember the time when I grieved that the night came so soon upon me, and obliged me for a few hours to shut out affluence and prosperity. I now seldom see the rising sun, but to " tell him," with the fallen angel, " how I hate his beams." I awake from sleep as to languor or imprisonment, and have no employment for the first hour but to consider by what art I shall rid myself of the second. I protract the breakfast as long as I can, because when it is ended I have no call for my attention, till I can with some degree of decency grow impatient for my dinner. If I could dine all my life, I should be happy; I eat not because I am hungry, but because I am idle: but alas! the time quickly comes when I can eat no longer; and so ill does my constitution second my inclination, that I cannot bear strong liquors: seven hours must then be endured before I shall sup; but supper comes at last, the more welcome as it is in a short time succeeded by sleep.

Such, Mr. Adventurer, is the happiness, the hope of which seduced me from the duties

N 4                              and

and pleafures of a mercantile life. I fhall be told by thofe who read my narrative, that there are many means of innocent amufement, and many fchemes of ufeful employment, which I do not appear ever to have known; and that nature and art have provided pleafures, by which, without the drudgery of fettled bufinefs, the active may be engaged, the folitary foothed, and the focial entertained.

THESE arts, Sir, I have tried. When firft I took poffeffion of my eftate, in conformity to the tafte of my neighbours, I bought guns and nets, filled my kennel with dogs and my ftable with horfes; but a little experience fhewed me, that thefe inftruments of rural felicity, would afford me few gratifications. I never fhot but to mifs the mark, and, to confefs the truth, was afraid of the fire of my own gun. I could difcover no mufic in the cry of the dogs, nor could diveft myfelf of pity for the animal whofe peaceful and inoffenfive life was facrificed to our fport. I was not, indeed, always at leifure to reflect upon her danger; for my horfe, who had been bred to the chace, did not always regard my choice either of fpeed or way, but leaped hedges and ditches at his own difcretion, and hurried me along with the dogs, to the great diverfion of my brother fportfmen. His eagernefs of perfuit once incited him to fwim a river; and I had lei-

fure

sure to resolve in the water, that I would never hazard my life again for the destruction of a hare.

I THEN ordered books to be procured, and by the direction of the vicar had in a few weeks a closet elegantly furnished. You will, perhaps, be surprised when I shall tell you, that when once I had ranged them according to their sizes, and piled them up in regular gradations, I had received all the pleasure which they could give me. I am not able to excite in myself any curiosity after events which have been long passed, and in which I can, therefore, have no interest: I am utterly unconcerned to know whether TULLY or DEMOSTHENES excelled in oratory, whether HANNIBAL lost Italy by his own negligence or the corruption of his countrymen. I have no skill in controversial learning, nor can conceive why so many volumes should have been written upon questions, which I have lived so long and so happily without understanding. I once resolved to go through the volumes relating to the office of justice of the peace, but found them so crabbed and intricate, that in less than a month I desisted in despair, and resolved to supply my deficiences by paying a competent salary to a skilful clerk.

I AM naturally inclined to hospitality, and for some time kept up a constant intercourse of visits

with

with the neighbouring gentlemen : but though they are eafily brought about me by better wine than they can find at any other houfe, I am not much relieved by their converfation ; they have no fkill in commerce or the ftocks, and I have no knowledge of the hiftory of families or the factions of the country; fo that when the firft civilities are over, they ufually talk to one another, and I am left alone in the midft of the company. Though I cannot drink myfelf, I am obliged to encourage the circulation of the glafs ; their mirth grows more turbulent and obftreperous ; and before their merriment is at an end, I am fick with difguft, and, perhaps, reproached with my fobriety, or by fome fly infinuations infulted as a cit.

Such, Mr. Adventurer, is the life to which I am condemned by a foolifh endeavour to be happy by imitation ; fuch is the happinefs to which I pleafed myfelf with approaching, and which I confidered as the chief end of my cares and my labours. I toiled year after year with chearfulnefs, in expectation of the happy hour in which I might be idle ; the privilege of idlenefs is attained, but has not brought with it the bleffing of tranquillity.

T　　　I am,

Yours, &c.

Mercator.

NUMB. 103. TUESDAY, October 30, 1753.

—————————*Quid enim ratione timemus,*
*Aut cupimus?* ————— ———     JUV.

'How void of reason are our hopes and fears!
              DRYDEN.

IN those remote times when, by the intervention of FAIRIES, men received good and evil, which succeeding generations could expect only from natural causes, SOLIMAN, a mighty prince, reigned over a thousand provinces in the distant regions of the east. It is recorded of SOLIMAN, that he had no favourite; but among the principal nobles of his court was OMARADDIN.

OMARADDIN had two daughters, ALMERINE and SHELIMAH. At the birth of ALMERINE, the fairy ELFARINA had presided; and, in compliance with the importunate and reiterated request of the parents, had endowed her with every natural excellence both of body and mind, and decreed that " she should be sought in " marriage by a sovereign prince."

WHEN the wife of OMARADDIN was pregnant with SHELIMAH, the fairy ELFARINA was again invoked; at which FARIMINA, another power of the aerial kingdom, was offended.

FARIMINA

FARIMINA was inexorable and cruel; the number of her votaries, therefore, was few. ELFARINA was placable and benevolent; and FAIRIES of this character were observed to be superior in power, whether because it is the nature of vice to defeat its own purpose, or whether the calm and equal tenor of a virtuous mind prevents those mistakes, which are committed in the tumult and precipitation of outrageous malevolence.    But FARIMINA, from whatever cause, resolved that her influence should not be wanting; she, therefore, as far as she was able, precluded the influence of ELFARINA, by first pronouncing the incantation which determined the fortune of the infant, whom she discovered by divination to be a girl. FARIMINA, that the innocent object of her malice might be despised by others, and perpetually employed in tormenting herself, decreed, "that her person should be "rendered hideous by every species of deformity, "and that all her wishes should spontaneously "produce an opposite effect."

THE parents dreaded the birth of the infant under this malediction, with which ELFARINA had acquainted them, and which she could not reverse. The moment they beheld it, they were solicitous only to conceal it from the world; they considered the complicated deformity of unhappy SHELIMAH, as some reproach to themselves;
and

and as they could not hope to change her appearance, they did not find themselves interested in her felicity. They made no request to EL-FARINA, that she would by any intellectual endowment alleviate miseries which they should not participate, but seemed content that a being so hideous should suffer perpetual disappointment; and, indeed, they concurred to injure an infant which they could not behold with complacency, by sending her with only one attendant to a remote castle which stood on the confines of a wood.

ELFARINA, however, did not thus forsake innocence in distress; but to counterbalance the evils of obscurity, neglect, and ugliness, she decreed, that " to the taste of SHELIMAH the " coarsest food should be the most exquisite " dainty; that the rags which covered her, " should in her estimation be equal to cloth of " gold; that she should prize a palace less than " a cottage; and that in these circumstances " love should be a stranger to her breast." To prevent the vexation which would arise from the continual disappointment of her wishes, appeared at first to be more difficult; but this was at length perfectly effected by endowing her with CONTENT.

WHILE SHELIMAH was immured in a remote castle, neglected and forgotten, every city in the
dominions

dominions of SOLIMAN contributed to decorate the person, or cultivate the mind of ALMERINE. The house of her father was the resort of all who excelled in learning of whatever class; and as the wit of ALMERINE was equal to her beauty, her knowledge was soon equal to her wit.

THUS accomplished, she became the object of universal admiration; every heart throbbed at her approach, every tongue was silent when she spoke; at the glance of her eye every cheek was covered with blushes of diffidence or desire, and at her command every foot became swift as that of the roe. But ALMERINE, whom ambition was thus jealous to obey, who was reverenced by hoary wisdom, and beloved by youthful beauty, was perhaps the most wretched of her sex. Perpetual adulation had made her haughty and fierce; her penetration and delicacy rendered almost every object offensive; she was disgusted with imperfections which others could not discover; her breast was corroded by detestation, when others were softened by pity; she lost the sweetness of sleep by the want of exercise, and the relish of food by continual luxury: but her life became yet more wretched, by her sensibility of that passion, on which the happiness of life is believed chiefly to depend.

NOURASSIN,

NOURASSIN, the phyſician of SOLIMAN, was of noble birth, and celebrated for his ſkill through all the Eaſt.  He had juſt attained the meridian of life; his perſon was graceful, and his manner ſoft and inſinuating.   Among many others, by whom ALMERINE had been taught to inveſtigate nature, NOURASSIN had acquainted her with the qualities of trees and herbs.  Of him ſhe learned, how an innumerable progeny are contained in the parent plant; how they expand and quicken by degrees; how from the ſame ſoil each imbibes a different juice, which riſing from the root hardens into branches above, ſwells into leaves, and flowers, and fruits, infinitely various in colour, and taſte, and ſmell : of power to repel diſeaſes, or precipitate the ſtroke of death.

WHETHER by the caprice which is common to violent paſſions, or whether by ſome potion which NOURASSIN found means to adminiſter to his ſcholar, is not known; but of NOURASSIN ſhe became enamoured to the moſt romantic exceſs.   The pleaſure with which ſhe had before reflected on the decree of the FAIRY, " that ſhe " ſhould be ſought in marriage by a ſovereign " prince," was now at an end.   It was the cuſtom of the nobles to preſent their daughters to the king, when they entered their eighteenth year; an event which ALMERINE had often anticipated with impatience and hope, but now
wiſhed

wifhed to prevent with folicitude and terror. The period, urged forward, like every thing future, with filent and irrefiftible rapidity, at length arrived. The curiofity of SOLIMAN had been raifed, as well by accidental enco-miums, as by the artifices of OMARADDIN, who now hafted to gratify it with the utmoft anxiety and perturbation : he difcovered the confufion of his daughter, and imagined that it was produced like his own, by the uncer-tainty and importance of an event, which would be determined before the day fhould be paffed. He endeavoured to give her a peaceful confidence in the promife of the FAIRY, which he wanted himfelf; and perceived, with regret, that her diftrefs rather increafed than diminifhed : this incident, however, as he had no fufpicion of the caufe, only rendered him more impatient of delay; and ALMERINE, covered with ornaments by which art and na-ture were exhaufted, was, however reluctant, introduced to the king.

SOLIMAN was now in his thirtieth year. He had fate ten years upon the throne, and for the fteadinefs of his virtue had been furnamed the -JUST. He had hitherto confidered the gratifica-tion of appetite as a low enjoyment, allotted to weaknefs and obfcurity; and the exercife of he-roic virtue, as the fuperior felicity of eminence and power. He had as yet taken no wife; nor
had

had he immured in his palace a multitude of unhappy beauties, in whom defire had no choice,
and affection no object, to be fucceffively forfaken after unrefifted violation, and at laft fink
into the grave without having anfwered any
nobler purpofe, than fometimes to have gratified
the caprice of a tyrant, whom they faw at no
other feafon, and whofe prefence could raife
no paffion more remote from deteftation than
fear.

Such was Soliman; who, having gazed fome
moments upon Almerine with filent admiration, rofe up, and turning to the princes who
ftood round him, "To-morrow," faid he, "I
"will grant the requeft which you have fo often
"repeated, and place a beauty upon my throne,
"by whom I may tranfmit my dominion to
"pofterity: to-morrow, the daughter of Oma-
"raddin fhall be my wife."

The joy with which Omaraddin heard this
declaration, was abated by the effect which it
produced upon Almerine: who, after fome
ineffectual ftruggles with the paffions which agitated her mind, threw herfelf into the arms of
her women, and burft into tears. Soliman immediately difmiffed his attendants; and taking
her in his arms, enquired the caufe of her diftrefs: this, however, was a fecret, which neither
her pride nor her fear would fuffer her to reveal.

She

She continued filent and inconfolable; and
SOLIMAN, though he fecretly fufpected fome
other attachment, yet appeared to be fatisfied
with the fuggeftions of her father, that her
emotion was only fuch as is common to the fex
upon any great and unexpected event. He defifted from farther importunity, and commanded
that her women fhould remove her to a private
apartment of the palace, and that fhe fhould be
attended by his phyfician NOURASSIN.

NUMB. 104. SATURDAY, *November* 3, 1753.

———————————*Semita certe*
*Tranquillæ per virtutem patet unica vitæ.* JUV.
But only virtue fhews the paths of peace.

NOURASSIN, who had already learned
what had happened, found his defpair relieved by this opportunity of another interview.
The lovers, however, were reftrained from con-
dolence and confultation, by the prefence of the
women who could not be difmiffed : but NOU-
RASSIN put a fmall vial into the hand of ALME-
RINE as he departed, and told her, that it contained a cordial, which, if adminiftered in time,
would infallibly reftore the chearfulnefs and
vigour

vigour that she had lost. These words were heard by the attendants, though they were understood only by ALMERINE; she readily comprehended, that the portion she had received was poison, which would relieve her from languor and melancholy by removing the cause, if it could be given to the king before her marriage was compleated. After NOURASSIN was gone, she sate ruminating on the infelicity of her situation, and the dreadful events of the morrow, till the night was far spent; and then, exhausted with perturbation and watching, she sunk down on the sofa, and fell into a deep sleep.

THE king, whose rest had been interrupted by the effects which the beauty of ALMERINE had produced upon his mind, rose at the dawn of day; and sending for her principal attendant who had been ordered to watch in her chamber, eagerly enquired what had been her behaviour, and whether she had recovered from her surprise. He was acquainted, that she had lately fallen asleep; and that a cordial had been left by NOURASSIN, which he affirmed would, if not too long delayed, suddenly recover her from languor and dejection, and which, notwithstanding, she had neglected to take. SOLIMAN derived new hopes from this intelligence; and that she might meet him at the hour of marriage, with the chearful vivacity which the cordial of NOURASSIN would inspire,

spire, he ordered that it should, without asking her any question, be mixed with whatever she first drank in the morning.

ALMERINE, in whose blood the long-continued tumult of her mind had produced a feverish heat, awaked parched with thirst, and called eagerly for sherbet: her attendant, having first emptied the vial into the bowl, as she had been commanded by the king, presented it to her, and she drank it off. As soon as she had recollected the horrid business of the day, she missed the vial, and in a few moments she learned how it had been applied. The sudden terror which now seized her, hastened the effect of the poison; and she felt already the fire kindled in her veins, by which in a few hours she would be destroyed. Her disorder was now apparent, though the cause was not suspected: NOURASSIN was again introduced, and acquainted with the mistake; an antidote was immediately prepared and administered; and ALMERINE waited the event in agonies of body and mind, which are not to be described. The internal commotion every instant increased; sudden and intolerable heat and cold succeeded each other; and in less than an hour, she was covered with a leprosy; her hair fell, her head swelled, and every feature in her countenance was distorted. NOURASSIN, who was doubtful of the event, had withdrawn

to

to conceal his confusion; and ALMERINE, not knowing that these dreadful appearances were the presages of recovery, and shewed that the fatal effects of the poison were expelled from the citadel of life, conceived her dissolution to be near, and in the agony of remorse and terror earnestly requested to see the king. SOLIMAN hastily entered her apartment, and beheld the ruins of her beauty with astonishment, which every moment increased, while she discovered the mischief which had been intended against him, and which had now fallen upon her own head.

SOLIMAN, after he had recovered from his astonishment, retired to his own apartment; and in this interval of recollection he soon discovered that the desire of beauty had seduced him from the path of justice, and that he ought to have dismissed the person whose affections he believed to have another object. He did not, therefore, take away the life of NOURASSIN for a crime, to which he himself had furnished the temptation; but as some punishment was necessary as a sanction to the laws, he condemned him to perpetual banishment. He commanded that ALMERINE should be sent back to her father, that her life might be a memorial of his folly; and he determined, if possible, to atone by a second marriage for the errors of the first.

He

He confidered, how he might inforce and illuftrate fome general precept; which would contribute more to the felicity of his people, than
his leaving them a fovereign of his own blood;
and at length he determined to publifh this proclamation, throughout all the provinces of his
empire: " SOLIMAN, whofe judgment has been
" perverted, and whofe life endangered, by the
" influence and the treachery of unrivalled
" beauty, is now refolved to place equal defor-
" mity upon his throne; that, when this event
" is recorded, the world may know, that by
" VICE beauty became yet more odious than
" uglinefs; and learn, like SOLIMAN, to de-
" fpife that excellence, which, without VIRTUE,
" is only a fpecious evil, the reproach of the
" poffeffor, and the fnare of others."

SHELIMAH, during thefe events, experienced
a very different fortune. She remained, till
fhe was thirteen years of age, in the caftle; and
it happened that, about this time, the perfon to
whofe care fhe had been committed, after a fhort
ficknefs died. SHELIMAH imagined that fhe
flept; but perceiving that all attempts to awaken
her were ineffectual, and her ftock of pro-
vifions being exhaufted, fhe found means to
open the wicket, and wander alone into the
wood. She fatisfied her hunger with fuch berries and wild fruits as fhe found, and at night,

not

not being able to find her way back, she lay down under a thicket and slept. Here she was awaked early in the morning by a peasant, whose compassion happened to be proof against deformity. The man asked her many questions; but her answers rather increasing than gratifying his curiosity, he set her before him on his beast, and carried her to his house in the next village, at the distance of about six leagues. In his family she was the jest of some, and the pity of others; she was employed in the meanest offices, and her figure procured her the name of Goblin. But amidst all the disadvantages of her situation, she enjoyed the utmost felicity of food and rest; as she formed no wishes, she suffered no disappointment; her body was healthful, and her mind at peace.

IN this station she had continued four years, when the heralds appeared in the village with the proclamation of SOLIMAN. SHELIMAH ran out with others to gaze at the parade; she listened to the proclamation with great attention, and, when it was ended, she perceived that the eyes of the multitude were fixed upon her. One of the horsemen at the same time alighted, and with great ceremony intreated her to enter a chariot which was in the retinue, telling her, that she was without doubt the person whom NATURE and SOLIMAN had destined to be their queen.

SHELIMAH

SHELIMAH replied with a fmile, that fhe had no defire to be great ; " but," faid fhe, " if your " proclamation be true, I fhould rejoice to be the " inftrument of fuch admonition to mankind ; " and, upon this condition, I wifh that I were " indeed the moft deformed of my fpecies." The moment this wifh was uttered, the fpell of FARIMINA produced the contrary effect : her fkin, which was fcaly and yellow, became fmooth and white, her ftature was perceived gradually to increafe, her neck rofe like a pillar of ivory, her bofom expanded, and her waift became lefs ; her hair, which before was thin and of a dirty red, was now black as the feathers of the raven, and flowed in large ringlets on her fhoulders ; the moft exquifite fenfibility now fparkled in her eye, her cheeks were tinged with the blufhes of the morning, and her lips moiftened with the dew ; every limb was perfect, and every motion was graceful.. A white robe was thrown over her by an invifible hand ; the crowd fell back in aftonifhment, and gazed with infatiable curio- fity upon fuch beauty as before they had never feen. SHELIMAH was not lefs aftonifhed than the crowd : fhe ftood a while with her eyes fixed upon the ground ; and finding her confufion increafe, would have retired in filence ; but fhe was prevented by the heralds, who having with much importunity prevailed upon her to enter the

chariot,

chariot, returned with her to the metropolis, presented her to SOLIMAN, and related the prodigy.

SOLIMAN looked round upon the assembly, in doubt whether to prosecute or relinquish his purpose ; when ABBARAN, a hoary sage, who had presided in the council of his father, came forward, and placing his forehead on the footstool of the throne ; " Let the King," said he, " accept the reward of virtue, and take SHE- " LIMAH to his bed. In what age, and in " what nation, shall not the beauty of SHELIMAH " be honoured ? to whom will it be transmitted " alone ? Will not the story of the wife of " SOLIMAN descend with her name ? will it " not be known, that thy desire of beauty was " not gratified, till it had been subdued ? that " by an iniquitous purpose beauty became " hideous, and by a virtuous wish deformity " became fair ?"

SOLIMAN, who had fixed his eyes upon SHE- LIMAH, discovered a mixture of joy and confusion in her countenance, which determined his choice, and was an earnest of his felicity ; for at that moment, LOVE, who, during her state of deformity, had been excluded by the fairy ELFARINA's interdiction, took possession of her breast.

THE nuptial ceremony was not long delayed, and ELFARINA honoured it with her prefence. When fhe departed, fhe beftowed on both her benediction ; and put into the hand of SHELIMAH a fcroll of vellum, on which was this infcription in letters of gold :

" REMEMBER, SHELIMAH, the fate of
" ALMERINE, who ftill lives the reproach of
" parental folly, of degraded beauty, and per-
" verted fenfe. Remember ALMERINE ; and
" let her example and thy own experience teach
" thee, that wit and beauty, learning, affluence,
" and honour, are not effential to human felicity;
" with thefe fhe was wretched, and without
" them thou waft happy. The advantages
" which I have hitherto beftowed, muft now
" be obtained by an effort of thy own : that
" which gives relifh to the coarfeft food, is
" TEMPERANCE ; the apparel and the dwelling
" of a peafant and a prince, are equal in the
" eftimation of HUMILITY ; and the torment
" of ineffectual defires is prevented, by the
" refignation of PIETY to the will of HEAVEN ;
" advantages which are in the power of every
" wretch, who repines at the unequal diftri-
" bution of good and evil, and imputes to
" NATURE the effects of his own folly."

THE King, to whom SHELIMAH communicated thefe precepts of the FAIRY, caufed
them

them to be tranfcribed, and with an account of
the events which had produced them diftributed
over all his dominions. Precepts which were
thus enforced, had an immediate and extenfive
influence; and the happinefs of SOLIMAN and
of SHELIMAH was thus communicated to the
multitudes whom they governed.

❖❖❖❖❖❖❖❖❖❖❖❖❖❖❖❖❖❖❖❖❖❖❖

NUMB. 105. TUESDAY, *November* 6, 1753.

*Novam comicam* MENANDRUS, *æqualefque ejus
ætàtis magis quam operis,* Philemon ac *Diphilus, &
invenere intra pauciſſimds annos, neque imitandam
reliquere.* VELL. PATERCUL.

MENANDER, together with Philemon and Diphilus, who muft be named with him rather as
his contemporaries than his equals, invented
within the compafs of a few years a new kind
of comedy, and left it beyond the reach of imitation.

### To the ADVENTURER.

SIR,

MORALITY, tafte, and literature, fcarcely
ever fuffered more irreparably, than by
the lofs of the comedies of. MENANDER; fome
of whofe fragments, agreeable to my promife, I
am now going to lay before you, which I fhould

imagine

imagine would be as highly prized by the curious, as was the COAN VENUS which APELLES
left imperfect and unfinifhed.

MENANDER was celebrated for the fweetnefs,
brevity, and fententioufnefs of his ftile.  " He
" was fond of EURIPIDES," fays QUINTILIAN,
" and nearly imitated the manner of this tragic
" writer, though in a different kind of work.
" He is a complete pattern of oratorial ex-
" cellence : ità omnem vitæ imaginem expreffit,
" tanta in eo inveniendi copia, & eloquendi fa-
" cultas; ità eft omnibus rebus, perfonis, af-
" fectibus, accommodatus : fo various and fo
" juft, are all his pictures of life ; fo copious is
" his invention, fo mafterly his elocution ; fo
" wonderfully is he adapted to all kinds of fub-
" jects, perfons, and paffions." This panegyric
reflects equal honour on the critic, and on the
comedian.  QUINTILIAN has here painted ME-
NANDER with as lively and expreffive ftrokes, as
MENANDER had characterized the Athenians.

BOILEAU, in his celebrated eighth fatire, has
not reprefented the mifery and folly of man, fo
forcibly or humoroufly as MENANDER.

Ἅπαντα τὰ ζῶ᾽ ἔςι μακαριώτερα,
Καὶ νοῦν ἔχοντα μᾶλλον ἀνθρώπε πολύ.
Τὸν ὄνον ὁρᾶν ἔξεςι πρῶτα πετόνι,
Οὗτος κακοδαίμων ἐςιν ὁμολογεμένως.

Τίτῳ

Τέτῳ κακὸν δι᾿ αὐτὸν ἐδὲν γίγνεται,
Ἀ δὲ φύσις δίδωκεν αὐτῳ ταυτ᾿ ἔχει.
Ἡμεῖς δὲ χωρὶς τῶν ἀναγκαίων κακῶν,
Αὐτοὶ παρ᾿ αὐτῶν ἕτερα προστοριζομεν.
Λυπούμεθ᾿, ἂν πταρῃ τίς· ἂν εἴπῃ κακῶς,
Ὀργιζόμεθ᾿· ἂν ἴδῃ τίς ἐνύπνιον, σφόδρα
Φοβούμεθ᾿· ἂν γλαὺξ ἀνακράγῃ δεδοίκαμεν·
Ἀγωνίαι, δόξαι, Φιλοτιμίαι, νόμοι,
Ἅπαντα ταῦτ᾿ ἐπίθετα τῇ φύσει κακά.

" All animals are more happy, and have more
" underftanding than man. Look, for inftance,
" on yonder afs ; all allow him to be miferable :
" his evils, however, are not brought on him
" by himfelf and his own fault: he feels only
" thofe which nature has inflicted. We, on the
" contrary, befides our neceffary ills, draw upon
" ourfelves a multitude of others. We are me-
" lancholy, if any perfon happen to fneeze; we
" are angry, if any fpeak reproachfully of us ;
" one man is affrighted with an unlucky dream,
" another at the hooting of an owl. Our con-
" tentions, our anxieties, our opinions, our
" ambition, our laws, are all evils, which we
" ourfelves have fuperadded to nature." Com-
parifons betwixt the conditions of the brutal and
human fpecies, have been frequently drawn ;
but this of MENANDER, as it probably was the
firft, fo it is the beft I have ever feen.

Iɪ

IF this paſſage is admirable for the vivacity and ſeverity of its ſatire, the following certainly deſerves deeper attention for weight of ſentiment, and ſublimity and purity of moral.

Εἴ τις δὲ θυσίαν προσφέρον, ὦ Πάμφιλε,
Ταύρων τε πλῆθ☾ ἢ ἐρίφων, ἢ, νη Δία,
Ἑτέρων τοιύτων, ἢ κατασκεύασματα
Χρυσας ποιήσας χλαμύδ☾ ἤτοι πορφυρὰς,
Ἢ δἰ ἐλέφαντος, ἢ σμαράγδυ ζώδια,
Εὖνυν νομίζει τόν Θεὸν καθισάναι,
Πλανατ' ἐκεῖν☾, καὶ φρένας κύφας ἔχει.
Δεῖ γὰρ τὸν ἄνδρα χρήσιμον πεφυκέναι,
Μὴ παρθένυς φθείροντα, μὴ μοιχώμενον,
Κλέπτοντα, καὶ σφάτJοντα χρημάτων χάριν.
Μηδὲ βελόνης ἔναμμ' ἐπιθυμης Πάμφιλε,
Ὁ γαρ Θεος βλέπει σὲ πλησίον παρών.

"He that offers in ſacrifice, O Pamphilus, a
"multitude of bulls and of goats, of golden
"veſtments, or purple garments, or figures of
"ivory, or precious gems ; and imagines by this
"to conciliate the favour of GOD, is groſsly
"miſtaken, and has no ſolid underſtanding.
"For he that would ſacrifice with ſucceſs, ought
"to be chaſte and charitable, no corrupter of
"virgins, no adulterer, no robber or murderer
"for the ſake of lucre.    Covet not, O Pam-
"philus, even the thread of another man's
                                    "needle;

" needle; for GOD, who is near thee, per-
" petually beholds thy actions."

TEMPERANCE, and justice, and purity, are
here inculcated in the strongest manner, and upon
the most powerful motive, the OMNISCIENCE of
the DEITY; at the same time superstition and
the idolatry of the heathen are artfully ridiculed.
I know not among the ancients any passage that
contains such exalted and spiritualized thoughts
of religion. Yet if these refined sentiments were
to be inserted in a modern comedy, I fear they
would be rejected with disdain and disapproba-
tion. The Athenians could endure to hear
GOD and VIRTUE mentioned in the theatre;
while an English and a CHRISTIAN audience
can laugh at adultery as a jest, think obscenity
wit, and debauchery amiable. The murderer,
if a duellist, is a man of honour, the gamester
understands the art of living, the knave has penetration and knows mankind, the spendthrift is
a fellow of fine spirit, the rake has only robbed a
fresh country girl of her innocence and honour,
the jilt and the coquet have a great deal of vivacity and fire; but a faithful husband is a dupe
and a cuckold, and a plain country gentleman a
novice and a fool. The wretch that dared to
ridicule SOCRATES abounds not in so much
false satire, ribaldry, obscenity, and blasphemy,

as

as our witty and wicked triumvirate, WYCHER-
LEY, CONGREVE, and VANBRUGH.

MENANDER has another very remarkable reflection, worthy even that divine religion, which
the laſt-mentioned writers ſo impotently endeavoured to deride. It relates to the forgiveneſs
of enemies, a precept not totally unknown to
the ancient ſages, as hath raſhly been affirmed ;
though never inculcated with ſuch frequency,
fervor and cogency, and on motives ſo weighty
and efficacious, as by the founder of the CHRIS-
TIAN SYSTEM.

Οὗτῷ κράτιςῷ ἐς᾽ ἀνὴρ, ὦ Γοργία,
Ὅςις ἀδικεῖσθαι πλεῖς᾽ ἐπίςαται βροτῶν.

" He, O Gorgias, is the moſt virtuous man,
" who beſt knows among mortals how to bear
" injuries with patience."

IT may not be improper to alleviate the ſeri-
ouſneſs of theſe moral reflections, by the addition
of a paſſage of a more light and ſprightly turn.

Ὁ μεν Ἐπιχάρμῷ τὰς Θεὰς εἶναι λέγει,
Ἀνέμας, ὕδωρ, γῆν, ἥλιον, πῦρ, ἄςερας·
Ἐγὼ δ᾽ ὑπέλαβον χρησίμας εἶναι Θεὰς
Τ᾽ ἀργύριον ἡμῖν καὶ τὸ χρυσίον μόνον.
Ἱδρυσάμενῷ τὰτε, γὰρ εἰς τὴν οἴκιαν
Εὖξαι τὶ βάλει, πάντα σοὶ γενήσεται,
Ἀγρος, οἴκιαι, θεράποντες, ἀργυρώματα,
Φίλοι, δικαςαὶ, μάρτυρες——

4                                    " Epi-

" Epicharmus, indeed, calls the winds, the wa-
" ter, the earth, the sun, the fire, and the stars,
" Gods. But I am of opinion that gold and
" silver are our only powerful and propitious
" deities. For when once you have introduced
" these into your house, wish for what you will,
" you shall quickly obtain it ; an estate, a habi-
" tation, servants, plate, friends, judges, wit-
" nesses."

FROM these short specimens, we may in some
measure be enabled to judge of MENANDER's
way of thinking and of writing ; remembering
always how much his elegance is injured by a
plain prosaic translation, and by considering the
passages singly and separately, without knowing
the characters of the personages that spoke
them, and the aptness and propriety with which
they were introduced.

THE delicacy and decorum observed constantly
by MENANDER, rendered him the darling writer
of the Athenians, at a time when the Athenians
were arrived at the height of prosperity and politeness, and could no longer relish the coarse
railleries, the brutal mirth, and illiberal wit, of
an indecent ARISTOPHANES. " MENANDER,"
says PLUTARCH, " abounds in a precious Attic
" salt, which seems to have been taken from
" the same sea, whence Venus herself arose.
" But the salt of ARISTOPHANES is bitter,
" disgusting, and corrosive."

THERE

THERE are two circumſtances that may juſtly give us a mean opinion of the taſte of the Romans for comic entertainments : that in the Auguſtan age itſelf, notwithſtanding the cenſure of HORACE, they preferred the low buffoonery and drollery of PLAUTUS to the delicacy and civility of TERENCE, the faithful copier of MENANDER; and that TERENCE, to gratify an audience unacquainted with the real excellencies of the drama, found himſelf obliged to violate the ſimplicity of MENANDER's plots, and work up two ſtories into one in each of his comedies, except the excellent and exact HECYRA. But this duplicity of fable abounding in various turns of fortune, neceſſarily draws off the attention from what ought to be its chief object in a legitimate comedy, CHARACTER and HUMOUR.

I am, SIR,

Z

Your humble ſervant,

PALÆOPHILUS.

The End of the THIRD VOLUME.

www.ingramcontent.com/pod-product-compliance
Lightning Source LLC
Chambersburg PA
CBHW060554030726
47498CB00005B/1381